OTTAWA BOOK OF Everything

Everything you wanted to know about Ottawa and were going to ask anyway

Arthur Montague

MACINTYRE PURCELL PUBLISHING INC.

Copyright 2017 MacIntrye Purcell Publishing

All rights reserved. No part of this book covered by the copyrights hereon may be reproduced or used in any form or by any means – graphic, electronic, or mechanical – without the prior written permission of the publisher. Any request for photocopying, recording, taping, or information storage and retrieval systems of any part of this book shall be directed in writing to the Canadian Reprography Collective, 379 Adelaide Street, West, Suite M1, Toronto, Ontario, M5V 1S5.

MacIntyre Purcell Publishing Inc.
194 Hospital Rd.
Lunenburg, Nova Scotia
B0J 2C0
(902) 640-3350

www.macintyrepurcell.com
info@macintyrepurcell.com

Cover photo courtesy of Ottawa Tourism
Photos: Ottawa Tourism: page 8, 20, 36, 44, 64, 77, 96, 114, 154, 168, 182
istockphoto: page 6
Cover and Design: Channel Communications Inc.

Printed and bound in Canada by Marquis.

Library and Archives Canada Cataloguing in Publication
Montague, Art
The Ottawa Book of Everything /
Art Montague
ISBN 978-1-77276-081-1 Book
978-1-77276-082-8 Electronic Book
978-1-77276-083-5 Digital
Ottawa (Ont.). 2. Ottawa (Ont.)--Miscellanea. I. Title.
FC3096.18M65 2007   971.3'84
C2007-905135-9

MacIntyre Purcell Publishing Inc. would like to acknowledge the financial support of the Government of Canada and the Nova Scotia Department of Tourism, Culture and Heritage.

Introduction

Of course no one book can really be about everything, but we hope the *Ottawa Book of Everything* helps capture in some small way the essence of the city and its people. We really could have produced volumes full of facts, statistics, observational tid-bits, favourites, insights and outrages. In fact, our most difficult task by far was determining not what to write about, but rather, what to exclude.

Great cities are products of their contradictions, and thankfully Ottawa has them in abundance. We've explored the nooks and crannies, from the transformation from lumber town to G-town and capital city to the First Nations people to the waves of immigrants whose fingerprints are all over the new city. Tycoons, criminals, scandal and success, it is all here. And we throw in a dash of celebrity for good measure.

An amazing team worked on this project. Kelly Inglis coordinated much of the editorial. Samantha Amara, Kathleen Quinn, Charelle Evelyn, Randy Ray, Chris Robinson, Earl Miller, Corey Slumkoski and Rachel Eugster all offered their talents as researchers and writers. This book simply would not have happened without their insights, intelligence and skill.

Last, but certainly not least, I am greatly indebted to the Ottawans who took time out of often jam-packed schedules to mine their Ottawa experiences and provide us with some truly delightful top five lists.

Hope you have as much fun reading this as we did putting it together.

— Arthur Montague

Table of Contents

INTRODUCTION 3

OTTAWA, OUR NATION'S HOMETOWN 7

TIMELINE 9
From 12,000 Before Present to Today . . . Control of the River . . . Philemon Wright founds Wrightsville . . . Construction of the Rideau . . . Canal . . . Bytown . . . The Capital is Chosen . . . Burn Baby Burn . . . Ottawa International Airport . . . Centennial Flame . . . Ottawa . . . Amalgamates . . . Royal Visit . . . Powerful earthquake . . . Senate Scandal

OTTAWA ESSENTIALS 21
From the Origin of the Name to Population Trends . . . Five Essential Ottawa Reads . . . G-Town . . . You Know You're From Ottawa When . . . Death and Marriage . . . Family Structure . . . Colleges and Universities . . . Professional Sports Teams . . . Religion

BUREAUCRATESE 35
From Accountability to Whistle Blower, We Give You the Lowdown on Ottawa's Third Official Language

URBAN GEOGRAPHY 43
Three Rivers Run Through it . . . Barry Wellar's Top Five Residential Streets in Ottawa . . . Sally Coutts and Stuart Lazear's Five Favourite Heritage Structures . . . Going Green . . . Five Free Things to Do in Ottawa . . . Biking Country . . . Parliament Buildings . . . Living History

WEATHER 61
All Time Weather Winners . . . Ian Black's Top Five Severe Weather Events . . . Winterlude . . . Five Weather-Dependent Fun Activities . . . Ice Storm of '98 . . . Five Hottest . . . Coldest Days . . . Growing Seasons . . . When it Feels Worse than it is

CRIME AND PUNISHMENT 75
Ottawa Crimeline . . . Five Ottawa Cold Cases . . . In the Line of Duty . . . Serenity Shattered. . . The Senate Scandal: Mike Duffy . . . Parliamentary Power Corruptions . . . In a Day's Work . . . Firebomb Murder for Hire . . . Ron Cooper's Top Five Fraud Scams . . . The Sorry Cop . . . Drug Offences . . . Ottawa By-law services

CULTURE 93
Places You Must Be Seen . . . Alanis Morissette . . . Les DeMarbre's Five Best Places to Shoot . . . Canadian Tulip Festival . . . Five TV/Film Personalities From Ottawa . . . A Beaver Tale . . . Museum Central . . . Being Green . . . Get Stuffed

ECONOMY 109
From GDP to Taxes . . . Incomes . . . You Said How Much? . . . Gates Crasher . . . Just the Right Tool . . . Housing . . . The Tiger that Roared . . . Silicon Valley North . . . Jobs and More Jobs . . . Five Businesses to Watch . . . Technology Outlook . . . Agriculture

POLITICS 131
Municipal Government. . . . . Ottawa Mayors . . . Lady Charlotte . . . Keeping it in the Family. . . Women in Politics . . Ottawans Get Wise to Political Ploys . . .Voter Turnouts

THEN AND NOW 143
Population Then and Now . . . Trains to Nowhere . . . Lords of Lumber . . . A Capital Controversy . . . Thomas Ahern . . . Ottawa's Titanic Connection . . . Cross Roads . . . Hockey Town

FIRST PEOPLE 157
Population . . . Chief Tessouat . . . Speaking the Language . . . Creation Myth . . . Kirby Whiteduck's Five Historical Claims to Algonquin Territory . . . Lifestyle . . . Aboriginal Place Names . . . Victoria Island . . . Stepping into the Past

GO AHEAD, TAKE FIVE MORE 171
Ben Mulroney's Five Things You Don't Know About 24 Sussex Drive . . . Brian Kilrea's Favourite Hockey Players . . . Michael Haynes' Top Five Favourite Hiking Trails By Season . . . Art Montague Tells His Best Kept Secrets . . . Barb Fradkin's Five Murder Scenarios in the Nation's Capital . . . Jacquelin Holzman's Five Important Decisions that Shaped Ottawa . . . Rhys Phillips Weighs In on His Favouite Landmark Buildings

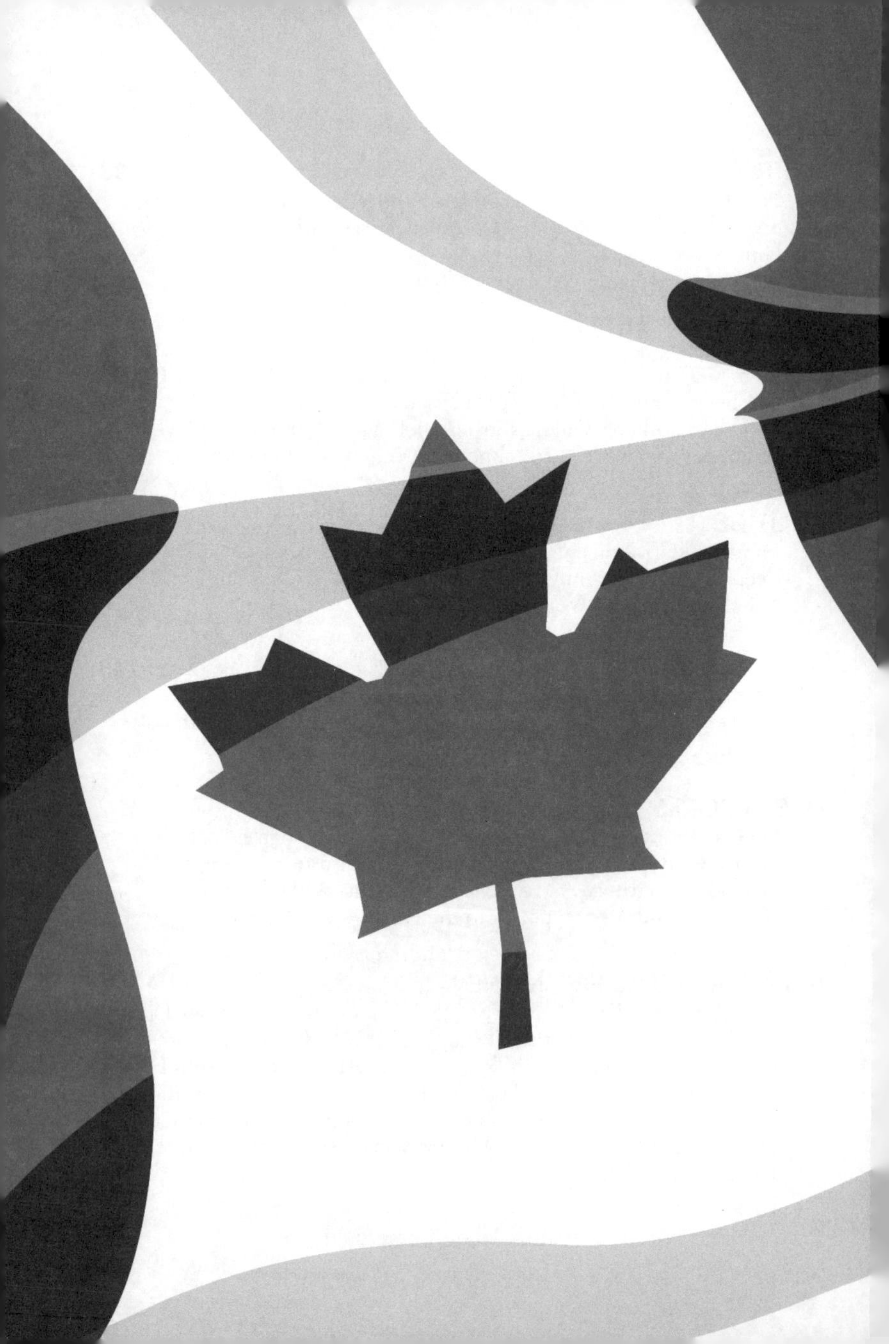

Ottawa, Our Nation's Hometown

Dominic D'Arcy is known as Ottawa's Singing Policeman. He has been a proud resident of the city since 1965 when he joined the Ottawa Police Service. When the city amalgamated in 2001, he felt it was time for Ottawa to have a new song.

D'Arcy, along with writers Dave McConnell and Robin Moir, wrote about Ottawa's rich history, beauty, its people, hope, understanding and pride. The result was an enduring message of love and peace.

When I look out upon the city from the Peace Tower on the Hill,
and see how much we've grown, and we're growing still.
It's a city with a heart that beats for me and you,
an eternal beacon burning strong, bright and true

Ottawa, Ottawa, we sing your name out loud.
Ottawa, Ottawa, you have made us so proud.
In this land of varied cultures we find our common ground
in Ottawa, Ottawa, our nation's hometown.

Many great leaders have held a seat at City Hall
and those who came before us helped to build it all.
They left us something special to embrace and to defend,
oh, this shining jewel, oh, this great land.

Ottawa, Ottawa, we sing your name out loud.
Ottawa, Ottawa, you have made us so proud.
In this land of varied cultures we find our common ground
in Ottawa, Ottawa, our nation's hometown.

Ottawa, Ottawa, chantons ton nom a voix claire.
Ottawa, Ottawa, on a raison d'être si fiers.
En ce pays de culture diverses, nous nous retrouvons la,
a Ottawa, Ottawa, notre capitale.

Ottawa, Ottawa, we sing your name out loud.
Ottawa, Ottawa, you have made us so proud.
In this land of varied cultures we find our common ground
in Ottawa, Ottawa, our nation's hometown.

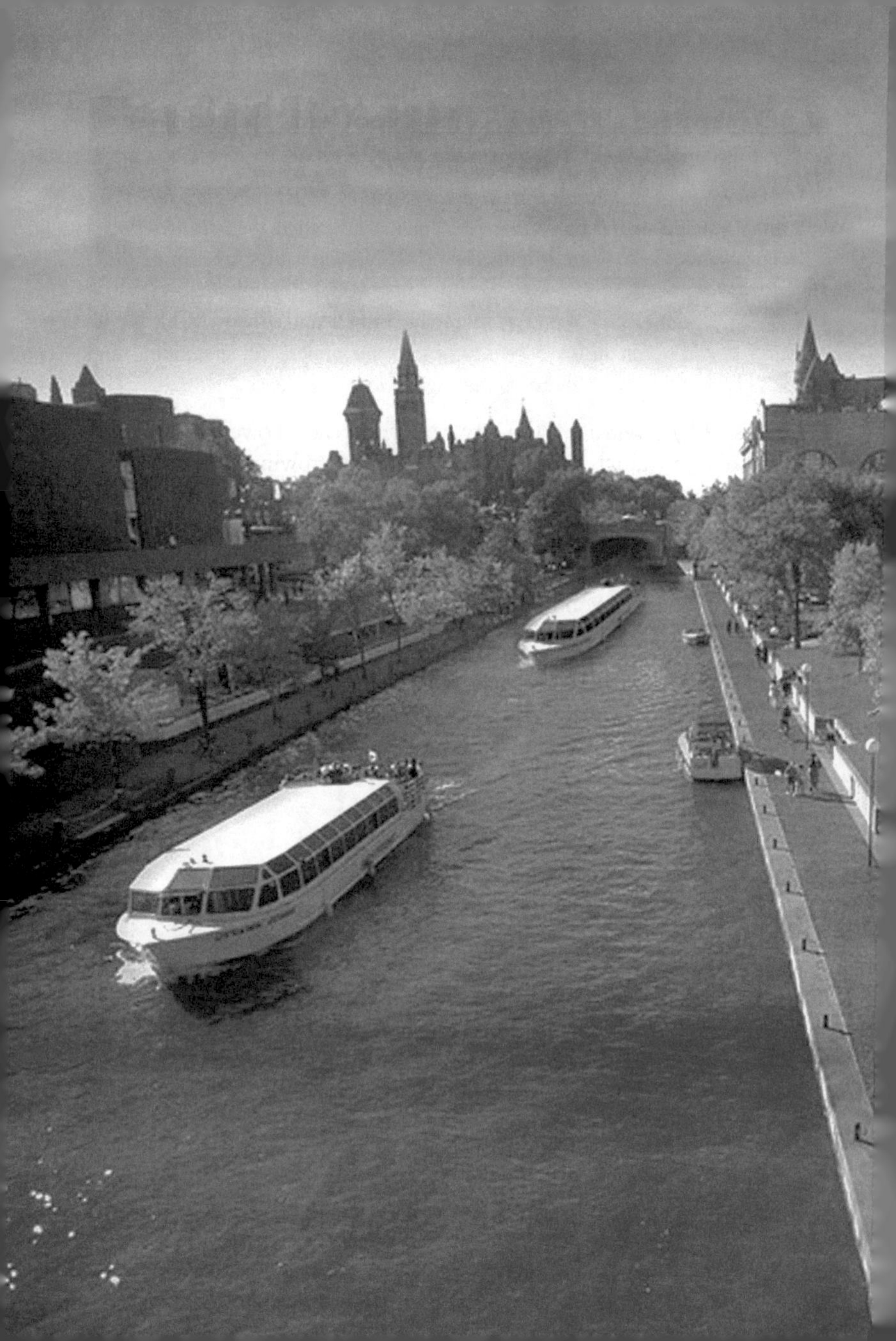

TIMELINE

Ottawa:

A Timeline

12,000 Before Present: Ice left from the great Ice Age disappears due to climatic changes and the area is eventually flooded to a depth of about 400 feet by an arm of the Atlantic Ocean, which forms an area scientists today call the Champlain Sea.

9,500 Before Present: The Champlain Sea retreats.

9,000 Before Present: Ancestors of the Algonquin tribes of eastern Canada and the United States follow game into areas recently vacated by ice and water.

4,000 Before Present: A culture called Laurentian establishes in eastern and southern Ontario.

1,000 Before Present: The Algonquin people migrate into the area now known as Ottawa.

1610: Étienne Brûlé is the first European to see the Chaudière Falls and the future site of the city of Ottawa.

1613: Samuel de Champlain passes the site of the future city of Ottawa.

1783: Lieutenant G. French explores the Rideau River from its mouth to its source.

1791: The Constitutional Act of 1791, passed by the British Parliament, establishes the individually administered regions of Upper and Lower Canada.

1793: Surveyor John Stegmann of York starts the survey of townships surrounding Ottawa.

1800: Philemon Wright founds Wrightsville (later Hull) on the north bank of the Ottawa River.

1809: Jehiel Collins and his family become the first settlers on the south side of the river.

1810: Braddish Billings establishes a homestead and becomes the first settler in Gloucester Township.

1821: Nicholas Sparks, one of Philemon Wright's farmhands, purchases 200 acres of land on the south shore of the Ottawa River for 95 pounds. The original Sparks property today includes the site of the parliament buildings and the downtown business district.

1823: Sir George Ramsay, the Earl of Dalhousie and Governor-in-Chief of British North America, purchases an extensive tract of land fronting the Ottawa River in preparation for the construction of the Rideau Canal.

1826: On September 26, Lieutenant Colonel John By and the Earl of Dalhousie choose the location for the entrance to the Rideau Canal and consequently found a community where the city of Ottawa exists today.

TIMELINE

1827: The name Bytown is first used to identify the community growing up around the Rideau Canal construction.

1827: Bytown's first school, the English Mercantile and Mathematical Academy, is established on Rideau Street.

1832: The construction of the Rideau Canal is complete and the population of Bytown reaches 1,000.

1836: Bytown's first newspaper, the *Bytown Independent and Farmer's Advocate*, appears.

1838: Thomas McKay, chief contractor of the Rideau Canal, builds Rideau Hall, later home of Canada's Governor General.

1841: The first election in Bytown for a seat in the Legislative Assembly of United Canada is held.

1843: William Harris founds the *Packet*, a weekly newspaper. In 1851, the *Packet* becomes the *Ottawa Citizen*.

1843: The Arch Riot takes place on August 20. Animosity between the Orangemen and Papists of Bytown erupts in fighting and stone throwing.

1845: On May 8, Élisabeth Bruyère and the Sisters of Charity establish a single ward hospital on Saint Patrick Street.

1849: The Stony Monday Riot takes place on September 17. Tories and Reformists clash over the planned visit of Lord Elgin. One man is killed while many more sustain injuries. Two days later, the two political factions, armed with cannons, muskets and pistols face off on the Sappers Bridge. The conflict is diffused by the military.

1850: The village of Bytown is incorporated as a town.

1854: Bytown is linked by rail with the larger centres of Toronto and Montréal.

1855: On January 1, Bytown is formally incorporated as a city. In gaining city status, Bytown adopts the name Ottawa.

1857: Queen Victoria chooses Ottawa as the capital of the Province of Canada.

Bytown

Born at Lambeth, England in 1779, Lt.-Col. John By was sent to Canada in 1826 as the military engineer in charge of the construction of the Rideau Canal, a monumental construction project designed to link the Ottawa River and Lake Ontario between Ottawa and Kingston by way of the Rideau and Cataraqui rivers.

The canal plan was hatched after the War of 1812 to provide a secure supply route from Montréal to Kingston, avoiding the vulnerable St. Lawrence River route. It involved the construction of more than 50 dams and 47 masonry locks over some 202 km, most of which was wilderness of rough bush, swamps and rock terrain.

Lt.-Col By also helped construct a town to house the men who worked on the canal. The resulting settlement, called Bytown, would later become known under the new name of Ottawa.

The Rideau Canal was completed in 1832 without the aid of modern construction equipment and was acclaimed as an engineering triumph. During an end-to-end tour of the finished canal in 1832, Lt.-Col. By was applauded for his achievement wherever he stopped. According to many engineering history scholars, By was "one of the greatest early engineers in Canada."

Upon his return to London, a surprised By faced accusations from

TIMELINE

1860: The Prince of Wales lays the cornerstone of the Centre Block of the Parliament Buildings on September 1.

1863: Ottawa's first professional police force is established.

1866: The Centre Block of the Parliament Buildings is completed, one year after the east and west blocks were finished.

1867: The British North America Act is ratified. Ottawa, with a population of 18,000, becomes the permanent capital of the Dominion of Canada.

---

the British Treasury Board that he had made a number of unauthorized expenditures en route to the completion of the £800,000 project. Rather than being honoured with the knighthood he expected, By was pilloried in the British press for excessive spending.

By spent the next years attempting to clear his name, but in 1836, at the age of only 53, he died. He died a broken man, his character still smeared. By would later be exonerated for any wrongdoing, but the damage was done.

By may have been maligned in his homeland, but in Canada, and particularly Ottawa, he is remembered fondly. The popular ByWard Market area in downtown Ottawa bears his name, as do Colonel By Secondary School and the scenic Colonel By Drive parkway that follows the first stretch of the canal through the city. A bronze statue in Major's Hill Park in downtown Ottawa overlooks the locks where the canal he helped build meets the Ottawa River.

In Ottawa, Colonel By Day is the name given to the Ontario civic holiday, which falls on the first Monday in August. Lt.-Col. By received national recognition in 1979 when Canada Post issued a stamp bearing his image to commemorate the bicentenary of his birth.

1868: On April 7, Thomas D'Arcy McGee is assassinated by James Patrick Whelan, Canada's first political assassination.

1869: James Patrick Whelan is found guilty of the murder of Thomas D'Arcy McGee and is hanged at the Nicholas Street Jail on February 11.

1874: Ottawa establishes a professional fire brigade.

1875: Ottawa households have running water, many years behind other Canadian cities.

1879: The Great Dominion Exhibition is held in Ottawa. Later the exhibition grounds become Lansdowne Park, named after the Marquis of Lansdowne, Governor General from 1883 to 1888.

1881: Ottawa's population exceeds 25,000.

1885: Electricity comes to Ottawa.

1886: The Central Experimental Farm is established on 1,196 acres of land beyond the city's southwestern limits.

1877: The telephone is first demonstrated to the Canadian public at the Ottawa Exhibition.

1877: Ottawa's first permanent city hall opens on Elgin Street.

1891: Electric streetcar service begins.

1895: Sparks Street between Elgin Street and Bank Street becomes Ottawa's first paved street.

TIMELINE

1900: A terrible fire decimates much of Hull and many buildings in Ottawa.

Burn Baby Burn

The *Ottawa Citizen* reported that just after 10 a.m., . . . a spark flew out of the chimney of (a) . . . wood-frame house in Hull and ignited a fire . . . The fire grew out of control and by noon had consumed most of downtown Hull . . . Embers borne by strong northerly winds ignited lumberyards on the Ontario shore . . . at 12:18 p.m. the alarm was sounded in Ottawa. At 3 p.m., buglers were sent . . . to call out the militia . . . explosions filled the air, as dynamite and industrial chemicals blew up. A power plant was burned, cutting electricity to whole sections of the city. Streetlights were off for five nights. Thousands of people filled the streets, anxious for news . . . By the time the fire burned itself out around midnight, Ottawa's industrial heart was gone."

On April 26th, 1900, a small house fire in Hull quickly turned into an inferno that destroyed much of Ottawa and Hull. Smoke from the fire could be seen as far away as Kingston.

In the end, over 14,000 people were left homeless. Miraculously, only seven people perished in the fire. Many people died later while living in grungy unsanitary tents.

Over 3,000 homes were destroyed and an estimated $100 million of property was lost. The Canadian Pacific Union Station was destroyed and Ottawa's lumber baron, J.R. Booth, lost his mansion along with 50 million feet of lumber.

The tragedy made international headlines and donations and support poured into Ottawa from around the world.

Fearful that many homeless people would flee Ottawa, the city acted swiftly to compensate victims. Nearly $1 million was paid out before the summer was over. By the end of the year, at least 750 new buildings had been built.

1907: The silent movie arrives in Ottawa with the first regular showings presented at Bennett's Vaudeville Theatre on Sparks Street.

1912: The Château Laurier Hotel and Union Station open for business.

1913: *Le Droit*, Ottawa's only French language daily newspaper, begins publishing.

1915: The Ottawa School Board is replaced by a three-member commission when it refuses to insist that teachers be qualified to speak English.

1916: The Parliament Buildings are severely damaged by fire, killing seven people.

1920: The Ottawa Air Station, Ottawa's first airport, opens at Rockcliffe.

1939: Montreal architect Ernest Cormier completes the Supreme Court of Canada building on Wellington Street west of Parliament Hill.

1947: Radio station CFRA begins broadcasting from founder Frank Ryan's farm at Baseline Road and Pinecrest.

1951: Charlotte Whitton is elected as Ottawa's first female mayor.

1954: Westgate, Ottawa's first shopping centre, opens on Carling Avenue.

1957: The Carleton University Act is approved, elevating Carleton College to university status.

1957: Queen Elizabeth II ignites the initial dynamite charge to launch construction of the Queensway, a 24-km expressway bisecting Ottawa.

TIMELINE

1960: Prime Minister John Diefenbaker opens the new Ottawa International Airport.

1960: Sparks Street between Elgin and Bank streets is closed to vehicular traffic for the summer months to permit the operation of a temporary pedestrian mall, Canada's first.

1961: Earnscliffe, the Ottawa residence of Sir John A. Macdonald and home of Britain's high commissioner to Ottawa, is declared a National Historic Site.

1961: Television station CJOH commences broadcasting on Channel 13.

1965: Prime Minister Lester B. Pearson raises the new red maple leaf flag on February 15 at Parliament Hill.

1965: The $13-million Macdonald-Cartier bridge spanning the Ottawa River between Ottawa and Hull, Quebec is opened.

1966: Eight people are killed and more than 50 injured when the Heron Road bridge collapses.

1967: On January 1, Canada's centennial year is officially launched when Prime Minister Lester Pearson lights the Centennial Flame at Parliament Hill.

1967: The 10,324-seat Civic Centre is completed at Lansdowne Park as home to the Ottawa 67's of the Ontario Hockey League.

1969: The Regional Municipality of Ottawa-Carleton is born with responsibility for 1,100 square miles and a population of 410,000.

1969: The largest hailstones ever measured in Ottawa fall on August 1. (Hailstones measure up to 2 3/4 inches in diameter.)

1981: U.S. President Ronald Reagan visits Ottawa; US agrees to ease social security eligibility claims for those who have worked in both countries.

1988: The National Arts Centre sells 16,408 seats for the British musical CATS, the largest single-day sale of tickets for a musical in Canada.

1990: The first world ice hockey tournament for women is held in Ottawa.

1992: After a 60-year absence from the NHL, the Ottawa Senators return to the National Hockey League.

1998: An ice storm coats Ottawa and eastern Ontario knocking out power to thousands of homes and toppling trees across the city and surrounding area.

2001: The city of Ottawa approves the nation's toughest and most extensive anti-smoking bylaws, banning smoking in restaurants, bars, private clubs and legions.

2001: The new city of Ottawa is created with the amalgamation of 11 local municipalities. Population is 854,000.

2003: The National Hockey League's Ottawa Senators file for bankruptcy and are sold to Eugene Melnyk, CEO of the Biovail pharmaceutical company.

TIMELINE

2003: Ottawa software giant Corel Corp., known for its WordPerfect and CorelDRAW program, accepts a $97.6 million (US) offer from Vector Capital, a San Francisco venture capital firm.

2005: Ottawa celebrates its 150th anniversary.

2007: Larry O'Brien is elected mayor, replacing incumbent Bob Chiarelli.

2007: The Ottawa Senators make the Stanley Cup finals. Ottawa watches in rapt attention as the Sens fall to Anaheim in five games.

2009: Ottawa hosts the 2009 IIHF World Junior Championship in Ottawa. Team Canada defeated Sweden 5-1 to win their fifth consecutive gold medal, setting the single-game attendance record for the tournament with 20,380 fans in the stands.

2009: Barack Obama visits Ottawa for the first time as the new President of the United States.

2010: An earthquake of 5.0 magnitude rocks Ottawa. The most powerful earthquake in 45 years.

2015: Liberals win back 24 Sussex with Justin Trudeau's victory in October 2015.

2016: Judge clears Senator Mike Duffy of all charges around the Senate expense scandal.

2017: Ottawa takes center stage as Canada celebrates its 150th birthday.

OTTAWA ROADS

- 6,000 lane-kilometres of local roads
- Network of major collector roads
- Network of minor collector roads
- 1,974 lane-kilometres of roads, including:
  - Transitway, arterial and major collector roads
  - Within urban area
- 5,900 km of paved roads
- 800 km of gravel roads
- 475 roadway bridges
- 1,580 km of sidewalk
- 65 km of transitway
- 830 parks

ESSENTIALS

Ottawa Essentials

Location: The city of Ottawa stretches from the border with Arnprior in the west to Cumberland in the east, and from the Ottawa River to Burritt's Rapids on the Rideau River. Forming the major portion of the larger region of Ottawa-Gatineau and spanning the Ontario-Quebec border, the Ottawa area is Canada's fourth largest Census Metropolitan Area (CMA), after Toronto, Montreal and Vancouver, with an estimated combined population of more than 1.1 million.

Origin of Name: Derived from the Algonquin term adawe, "to trade," the name given to the tribe who controlled trade on the Ottawa River. The name of the Ottawa River was called Riviére des Outaouais on their first map produced by the French in 1702. Ottawa would be called first Bytown after Lt-Col. John By of the Royal Engineers. The name Ottawa was officially adopted in 1855.

Nickname: Nation's Capital

Motto: "Advance-Ottawa-En Avant" (Written in two official languages, it means "Advance.")

City Flower: Tulip

City Flag: Adopted in 2001 when eleven municipalities amalgamated into one new city. The green and blue backdrop represents the importance of the city's green spaces and waterways. The stylized 'O' logo in the center of the flag represents the city's vibrancy and forward movement. As the centrepiece, it represents Ottawa as the Nation's Capital. It was designed to have a subtle similarity to the maple leaf and parliament buildings. The white streamers stemming from the 'O' symbolize unity, harmony and working together towards a common goal.

Coat of Arms: Granted on September 15, 1954 and formally declared in use on January 1, 1955. Components include a shield, a wreath, supporters and the city's motto.

Dates of Incorporation: 1850 as Bytown; 1855 as the city of Ottawa; amalgamated in 2001

Time Zone: Eastern Standard Time

Area Code: (613)

Postal Codes: K1A, K1B, K1H, K1L, K1N,K1P, K1R, K1T, K1V, K1Y, K1Z, K2A, K2B, K2E, K2G

System of Measurement: Metric

Voting Age: 18

Drinking Age: 19

ESSENTIALS

Take 5: FIVE CITIES IN THE RUNNING
WHEN CANADA'S CAPITAL WAS NAMED IN 1857

1. **Toronto**
2. **Kingston**
3. **Ottawa**
4. **Montreal**
5. **Quebec**

Statutory Holidays: New Year's Day (January 1), Family Day (the third Monday in February), Good Friday (the Friday before Easter), Victoria Day (the Monday before May 25), Canada Day (July 1), Civic Holiday (the first Monday in August—Col. By Day), Labour Day (the first Monday in September), Thanksgiving Monday (the second Monday in October), Christmas Day (December 25) and Boxing Day (December 26).

Take 5: BARBARA CLUBB'S TOP FIVE
ESSENTIAL OTTAWA READS

Barbara Clubb is the City Librarian and CEO of the Ottawa Public Library and past president of the Canadian Library Association. She tells us her top five books that she feels provide valuable insight into Ottawa and its people.

1. ***Ottawa: a Literary Portrait*** by John Bell (Pottersfield Press, 1992)
2. ***Where Rivers Meet: an Illustrated History of Ottawa*** by Courtney Bond (Windsor Publications, 1984)
3. ***Capital Walks: Walking Tours of Ottawa*** by Katharine Fletcher (Fitzhenry & Whiteside, 2004)
4. ***The Private Capital: Ambition and Love in the Age of MacDonald and Laurier*** by Sandra Gwyn (McClelland and Stewart, 1984)
5. ***The Serpent's Egg*** by J. FitzGerald McCurdy (Saratime Publications, 2001)

Sister Cities: On January 1, 2000, 11 municipalities merged into what is now the city of Ottawa. Some of those previous municipalities, including the former city of Ottawa, entered into sister city relationships with various municipalities from around the world. Since amalgamation, the city of Ottawa has not entered into any new such agreements.

POPULATION

Area	Population	Share of metro population (%)
City of Ottawa	960,000	73
City of Gatineau	314,801	23.4
OMATO*	34,673	3.1
QMAG**	41,835	3.7

* OMATO: Ontario Municipalities Adjacent to Ottawa

** QMAG: Québec Municipalities Adjacent to Gatineau

Population in Perspective (GMA):

Ottawa:	**960,000**
Montreal:	4,060,700
Toronto:	6,129,900
Vancouver:	2,504,300
Calgary:	1,363,300

Did you know...

... that recent immigrants — those who settled here in the past 10 years — make up 22.6 percent of the population? Now 204,445 recent immigrants live in Ottawa-Gatineau, the fourth highest concentration in the country.

ESSENTIALS

G-Town

Much like the rest of North America in the 19th century, Ottawa was a decidedly blue collar town. Loggers and raftsmen literally nursed millions of logs down the Ottawa and Gatineau rivers to Montreal, where they would find markets on the eastern seaboard, and across the Atlantic. Indeed Ottawa was the centre for lumber milling and the square-cut timber industry in North America.

On December 31, 1857, Ottawa was unexpectedly dealt a hand that forever altered its course. Because it was a safe distance from marauding Americans, Ottawa was chosen as the capital of Upper and Lower Canada. The civil service was born, and Ottawa has had a love/hate relationship with it ever since.

Initially, blue-collar Ottawa had little time for the budding bureaucracy. John H. Taylor in his publication *Ottawa, An Illustrated History*, put it this way: "As for the locals, the civil servants . . . came to be regarded as favoured although inferior citizens in what was otherwise a working-man's town . . . They were a set of men who got high salaries for doing nothing."

From a few hundred workers in the early days, the number of employees of the Ottawa-based federal civil service grew to 30,069 in 1951. By 1961 it was 36,945 and today it is over 117,000. One in five working Ottawans work for the government. If you add in healthcare and social services, it reaches almost one in three.

Although periodically the civil service suffers reverses in employment, by and large it continues to grow unabated, giving the Ottawa economy a stability not found in the rest of the country. The research arms of the federal government have also nurtured the high technology industry. As one astute observer put it, if the nation's capital were in Nunavut, the high technology industry would follow it there. Such is the importance and the economic power of the government sector.

YOU KNOW YOU'RE FROM

- You know your public service friends not by name but by pay scale code
- You remember the Party Palace
- You think Alanis Morissette is Canada's greatest celebrity
- "Go Leafs go" means watching the autumn colours disappear in Gatineau Park
- You believe the 2007 Stanley Cup was rigged
- You believe lost pets are front page news
- You know the Lockmaster is a bar, not someone who installs your security system
- Meech Lake is a public beach, not Mulroney's legacy
- You went to the Canada rally before the 1995 referendum for fear you'd have to show a passport to go drinking in Hull
- You think Corel Draw and Word Perfect were the greatest software programs ever designed
- Gidday is a standard greeting, not a sign of inbreeding
- Five levels of government are just not enough
- You believe an entire level of government is needed to run a city's park system
- Going to Hull is a party plan, not an insult
- You get excited when the feds announce a new royal commission
- A beavertail is a pastry, not a sexist remark
- You've sailed across the Ottawa River to buy beer in a corner store in Quebec
- You have never eaten a falafel when sober
- You really hate tulips
- "Under construction" road signs don't post an end date
- You remember the old, bathtub sized urinals at the Château Lafayette tavern
- You'd rather listen to Max Keeping's newscasts than to Lloyd Robertson's
- You've never met anyone who's been fired
- Overtime is a hockey term, not a workplace term

ESSENTIALS

OTTAWA WHEN...

- You are proud to have a "hot" Governor General
- You have your father's job, and you hate it as much as he did
- You visit relatives you hate in hopes of scoring government contracts
- You know what a Shawarma is, and that it is delicious
- You know that the Palladium is the Corel Centre is Scotiabank Place
- You plan on attending the Ottawa Bluesfest, although it never seems to attract blues performers
- You studied computer science to make big bucks in Silicon Valley but ended up in Kanata
- You have nearly been run over by Margaret Trudeau
- You think Tom Green is the funniest man alive
- You believe that if a restaurant has a neon cactus in the window, it means fine dining
- A night on the town means driving to Montreal
- You know the Bare Fax tavern does not involve document transmission
- You get all teary-eyed when you remember expense accounts before the Liberals were defeated
- You'd hate to live in Toronto because you'd have to work too hard
- You think the humane society is the cat sanctuary on Parliament Hill
- You enjoyed the 1998 ice storm
- You're used to seeing 18 wheeler trucks driving on King Edward and Rideau St.
- You cringe every time someone comments on how clean the city is
- You remember when the Ottawa Senators played at the Civic Centre
- You bought your first beer at a Hull corner store
- You think Calgarians support bilingualism
- You refuse to eat fish caught in the Ottawa River
- You realize circuses have been banned because City Council can't handle competition
- You think your Nortel stock will someday regain its value.
- Your unemployed neighbours call themselves consultants between contracts

Population Density:
Ottawa: 316.6 people/km^2
Montreal: 898.1 people/km^2
Toronto: 4,149.5 people/km^2
Vancouver: 5,249 people/km^2
Calgary: 1,360.2 people/km^2
New York City: 27,000 people/km^2

Median Ages:
Women: 39.9
Men: 38.2

AGING

Although Ottawa's population is one of the youngest city populations in the country, in every age group other than people over the age of 55 the numbers are declining as a percentage of the population.

POPULATION BY AGE AND SEX for the GMA (Ottawa-Gatineau)

Age	Males	Females	Total
0-14	107,305	104,125	211,430
15-24	125,615	112,400	238,015
25-44	162,630	171,530	334,160
45-64	148,895	157,210	306,105
65+	68,350	88,530	156,880

Source: Statistics Canada.

Did you know...

. . . that Lt.-Col. John By was the judicial authority in early Bytown? By earned a reputation for his fairness and sense of humour in dealing with miscreants. Disputes he failed to resolve in chambers, he ordered settled in a boxing ring on Rideau Street.

ESSENTIALS

They Said It

Not surprisingly, the new capital provoked good and ill-natured comments.

1. **Essayist Goldwin Smith called the new capital** "*a sub-arctic lumber village converted by royal mandate into a political cockpit.*"

2. **Governor-General Lord Monck in a letter to the Rt. Hon. Edward Cardwell in London:** "*It seems like an act of insanity to have fixed the capital of this great country away from the civilization, intelligence and commercial enterprise of this province, in a place that can never be of importance and where the political section of the community will live in isolation and removed from the action of any public opinion.*"

3. **Anthony Trollope, the British novelist wrote:** "*I know no modern Gothic purer of its kind or less sullied with fictitious ornamentation, and I know no site for such a set of buildings so happy as regards both beauty and grandeur.*"

Life Expectancy at Birth:

	Ontario	Canada
Male	79	79
Female	84	83

Did you know...

... that 44.8 percent of people in Ottawa-Gatineau consider themselves bilingual in English and French?

Take 5 — TOP FIVE LANGUAGES SPOKEN IN OTTAWA'S CENSUS METROPOLITAN AREA

1. *English: 62.4 percent*
2. *French: 38.5 percent*
3. *Chinese: 3 percent*
4. *Arabic: 3.2 percent*
5. *Italian: 1.1 percent*

Source: Statistics Canada.

MARITAL STATUS (POPULATION 15 AND OVER)

- Percentage who are married: 46.4
- Percentage who are single: 53.6
- Percentage who are divorced: 8.1
- Percentage who are common-law: 10.9
- Percentage widowed: 5.3
- Percentage separated: 3.1

Source: Stats Can.

BIRTHS, DEATHS AND MARRIAGES (2006)

- 10,000 births
- 4,200 deaths
- 4,000 marriages

Did you know...

... that Enoch Walkley opened a brickyard in the community in 1802? In 1833, following the decline of the log cabin, he erected the first all-brick house in Bytown. With time and an increase in prosperity, brick and stone became the preferred building materials in Ottawa. Walkley Road, a busy east-west artery in south Ottawa, is named for Walkley.

ESSENTIALS

Take 5 TOP FIVE TOURIST DESTINATIONS
IN OTTAWA-GATINEAU

1. **ByWard Market**
2. **Casino du Lac-Leamy** (Gatineau)
3. **Parliament Hill**
4. **Canadian Museum of Civilization** (Gatineau)
5. **Canadian War Musuem**

Source: Ottawa Tourism.

FAMILY STRUCTURE

- Total families: 340,515
- Total couple families: 284,145
- Married couples: 224,940
- Common-law couples: 59,205
- Female lone-parent families: 44,155
- Male lone-parent families: 12,213

Source: Statistics Canada.

RELIGION

Religions Practiced in Ottawa-Gatineau

- Catholic: 38.4 percent
- Protestant: 25.1 percent
- No religious affiliation: 22.8 percent
- Muslim: 1 percent
- Jewish: 1.2 percent
- Buddhist: 1.3 percent
- Hindu: 1.4 percent

Source: Statistics Canada.

EDUCATION
- Number of schools in Ottawa Catholic School Board: 82
- Teaching Staff: 2,500
- Support Staff: 1,500
- Students: 38,800
- Number of schools in the Ottawa Carleton District School Board: 147
- Estimated number of teaching staff: 4,048
- Estimated number of support staff: 2,059
- Estimated number of students: 72,388

Sources: Ottawa-Carleton District School Board; Ottawa Catholic School Board.

EDUCATIONAL INSTITUTIONS:
- The University of Ottawa, with 42,700 students, and Carleton University, with 30,130 students, are Ottawa's primary large degree Granting facilities.
- Algonquin College is the city's third largest educational institution with 37,760 students.
- Université du Québec en Outaouais in Gatineau is part of the Université du Québec System. It has more than 5,500 full and part time students.

MEDICAL
Ottawa has four major hospitals. The Ottawa Hospital, consisting of the Civic, General and Riverside campuses, the Children's Hospital of Eastern Ontario, Queensway-Carleton Hospital and Montfort Hospital.

In addition, there are a number of specialized hospitals and clinics in the region, including the Royal Ottawa Hospital providing specialty mental care in Eastern Ontario and the Canadian Department of Defense military hospital.

The Ottawa Paramedic Service responds to more than 129,000 calls annually at a wide range of medical emergencies and fires, water rescues, industrial accidents, hazardous material incidents and police operations. Ottawa's 330 paramedics form an integral part of the city's emergency

ESSENTIALS

They Said It

> In the book Three Years in Canada, Lt.-Col John By's close associate in the construction of the canal, Scottish civil engineer John MacTaggart, described the colonel this way. "*[A man] who encountered all privations with wonderful patience and good humour. He could sleep soundly anywhere and eat anything, even raw pork.*"

preparedness team and are the sole medically certified providers of out of- hospital medical treatment. They service an area of 2,791 km^2.

Source: City of Ottawa Communications.

FAMILY DOCTORS
- 510 family physicians in Ottawa registered with the Ontario College of Family Physicians
- 480 pharmacists work in Ottawa
- 575 practicing dentists work in Ottawa

Sources: Ontario College of Pharmacists; Ontario College of Family Physicians; Ontario Dental Association.

SPORTS
Ottawa has three professional sports team. The Ottawa Senators of the National Hockey League, haven't won any Stanley Cups since their return to the NHL in 1992. During the 2014-15 season, the Senators overcame a 14-point deficit and qualified for the playoffs. They lost to the Canadiens in six games in the first round of the playoffs.

NEWSPAPERS
The city's major daily newspapers are the *Ottawa Citizen*, the *Ottawa Sun* and *Le Droit*, a French language daily. Weekly and monthly papers include the *Business Journal*, *Ottawa Xpress*, the *Epoch Times* and the *Hill Times*.

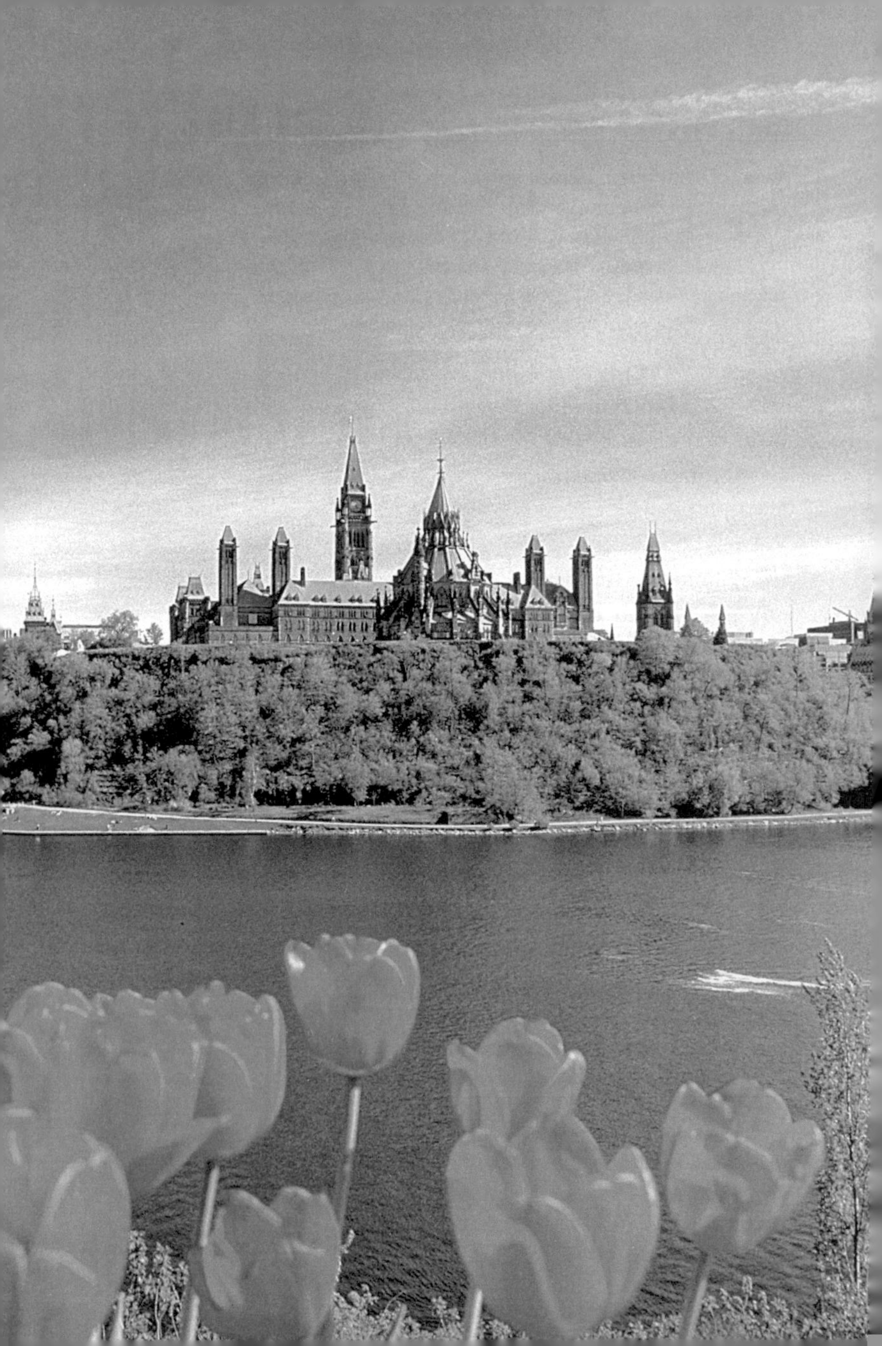

Bureaucratese:

Ever since Queen Victoria made her decision to choose Ottawa as the capital, there was a radical shift in the language of its citizens. Talk of logging and lumber changed to talk of peace, order and good government. Instead of discussions centring around a lumber baron's bottom line there was a new skill required in Ottawa, and that was reading between the lines. Here is a linguistic primer to help you along.

Accountability: Term employed when a civil servant fails to achieve deniability.

At this point in time: If a politician begins a sentence with these five words, it is not the start of a fairy tale. What it really means is that at any other point in time they have the option to have a completely different and often contradictory point of view.

Budgetary considerations: Politicians thrive on legislating benefits for citizens. Billion dollar programs are mere bagatelle to them since the legislation is meaningless without money. Unfortunately, "budgetary considerations" may prevent the Treasury Board from authorizing the money needed to provide the benefit.

Classified: Freedom of information doesn't mean all information. "Secret" and "Top Secret" are rubber stamps routinely used to ensure anonymity, mask ministerial gaffes, and, just incidentally, protect national security and sensitive interests.

Clearly: Politicians and bureaucrats share this term when they belly up to the trough of truth. What they mean is the opposite, but both firmly believe that if they say it, it "clearly" must be true.

Close of business: If work ends at 4:30, it is important to prepare by three. Earlier on Fridays, of course.

Community-based: Used when government reaches out to the people for grass roots decision-making. Of course, the available options for community-based decision making are provided by government. The term gained currency about the same time "participatory democracy" popped up like a bad penny.

Consensus: A stated means to resolve a matter by achieving unanimous agreement. While it usually reflects the lowest common denominator, it also has the value of spreading responsibility so thinly that no one will have to take the heat if things screw up.

Consultation: 1) A circuitous means to avoid making a decision or 2) a fishing expedition to drum up support for a decision already made.

Continuum: A gradual transition from one state to another without any major disruptions. Used to explain unexpected results. For example, it is just a blip on the continuum.

Cost sharing: A device employed by senior government to shift the expense of its more grandiose programs to junior governments. It enables the senior government to announce programs with much fanfare and favourable press, then blame the junior when it fails to pick up the tab.

BUREAUCRATESE

Data mining: Usually done by young turks looking to impress their political masters. It is the process of going through mounds of information with the sole purpose of finding any word, phrase or figure that could support a decision, or equally important to undermine a foe's integrity.

Deniability: A word that's only whispered. The practice insulates decision makers from the fallout of bad decisions, ensuring that accusatory fingers point not to cabinet ministers and other senior officials but to file clerks.

Directives: Formally written directions from on high that constitute the do's and don'ts of civil servanting. They cover everything from appropriate workplace dress to demeanor in the presence of royalty, i.e., ministers and their deputies.

Take 5: SEYMOUR MAYNE'S TOP FIVE PHRASES THAT DESCRIBE OTTAWA

Seymour Mayne is the author, editor and/or translator of more than fifty books including *El Viejo Sofá Azul*, short fiction in Spanish translation (Anábasis), *Ricochet* (Mosaic), a selection of his word sonnets, and a companion volume, *September Rain* (Mosaic), which recently received a Canadian Jewish Book Award. A University of Ottawa professor of Canadian literature and creative writing, he has supervised the publication of a series of more than twenty annual anthologies of new writing.

1. "Ottawa dozes amongst its leafy trees, gathers a green belt around its waist"
2. "Hunkers down and holds its own in encircling storm and snowdrift"
3. "After the third fall even the traffic falls away in the thick sinking snow"
4. "Ottawa rests laid back on its ridge of rock"
5. "Hear its whisper shaped out of a dozen accents"

Empowerment: A term often used to lull relatively powerless special interest groups into thinking someone in government is listening.

Evaluate: To spend money to see which is the best way to spend money.

Evaluation assessment: Perhaps this term may mean an evaluation is to be assessed. Not so, it's really just a job performance review.

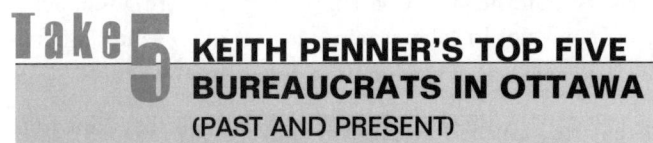

Take 5: KEITH PENNER'S TOP FIVE BUREAUCRATS IN OTTAWA (PAST AND PRESENT)

Keith Penner is a former parliamentarian and federal public servant. Currently, he is editor of "Beyond the Hill" the official publication of The Canadian Association of Former Parliamentarians. He also serves as Chairman of the Chartered Institute of Logistics and Transport (North America).

1. **Paul Tellier.** Served as Clerk of the Privy Council and Secretary to the Cabinet from 1985 to 1992. Prior to holding these positions, he held several senior government positions, including Deputy Minister of Indian Affairs and Northern Development and Deputy Minister of Energy, Mines and Resources. One of the most effective public servants in the history of Canada, he went on to become President and Chief Executive Officer of the Canadian National Railway Company, turning an inefficient Crown Corporation into a leading and highly profitable North American transportation company.

2. **Arthur Kroeger:** Joined the Department of External Affairs in 1958. In 1974, he was appointed Deputy Minister of Indian and Northern Affairs where he was responsible for initiating the Aboriginal Land Claims Process. He subsequently served as Deputy Minister in five other departments, including Transport, Energy and Employment and Immigration. A Westerner who rose to the top as a federal public servant, he has been described as Canada's "dean of deputy ministers."

BUREAUCRATESE

Formative: The gestation period for any new policy, plan or legislation. Can last for years or decades.

In the final analysis/at the end of the day/the bottom line: These are terms for "the decision has been made," "no more analysis is possible," "there is no tomorrow (on a particular issue)" and "there is no room at the end of the page."

---

3. **Moya Greene:** A Newfoundlander, Ms.Greene is President and Chief Executive Officer of Canada Post Corporation. She has been a senior officer in three large multinational companies, but also has a strong public sector background. As Assistant Deputy Minister, Policy, for Transport Canada, she was responsible for broad reform of the over-burdened transportation system; the privatization of CN; the deregulation of the Canadian airline industry; and the commercialization of the Canadian port system.

4. **Simon Reisman:** Joined the public service in 1946 working in the Department of Labour. In later years, he went on to serve as Secretary of the Treasury Board and then Deputy Minister of Finance. The Public Service of Canada has never had a better negotiator. In 1964, he spearheaded the team that negotiated the Auto Pact. After leaving the public service for awhile, he was called back in 1985 by Prime Minister Brian Mulroney to head Canada's negotiations that led to the Free Trade Agreement with the United States.

5. **Roger Roy:** While less often in the public eye, Roger Roy represented the best in the senior management ranks of the public service. He was a "behind-the-scenes" dedicated expert in the field of transportation economics. His work as an analyst produced annual reviews and reports on the state of the transportation sector in Canada. Both the users and the providers of transportation systems depended on this information to assist them in their decision-making.

In your corner: Loyal friends are somewhat of a rare commodity in Ottawa. To have them in your corner simply means they believe you can still do them some good.

It's a wash: Possibly deriving from "one hand washes the other," this phrase is often heard in the offices of the tax man. The politicians giveth, the tax man taketh away.

Linear: A mathematical term often used in the negative (non-linear) to explain the disparate and seemingly disassociated connections between finance and function.

Massaging: A special and highly prized skill in Ottawa. The ability to take otherwise meaningful material and neutralize it.

Negative increase/positive decrease: Only Statistics Canada people think they know what this means. The first means decrease and the second means increase.

New innovations: Introduced to replace "old innovations." Usually occurs when someone in authority decides to get proactive, most often over long lunches.

Optics: Scientifically, it has to do with the field and study of light. In Ottawa, it is used not to shine light on a particular issue but rather to deflect it by a variety of well-worn methods.

Out-source: Taking work outside of the sector where it can be done less expensively. In Ottawa, outsourcing is often done with retired and loyal civil servants or politicians.

Piggybacking: The process of dividing large consulting contracts and projects into individual segments to ensure dollar values are below the open bidding ceiling required to do the work.

Proactive: Get out ahead of the press corps.

BUREAUCRATESE

Raise a flag: Usually followed by burying the suspicious with mounds of paper, or better still, a report.

Restructuring: The reorganization of a department as a cost-saving measure.

Results-based management: Suggests, of course, that previous management was aimless. Results are often determined at strategic planning sessions.

Standing offer: An official pre-approval measure by which certain consulting firms have the inside track on contracts for government work.

Strategic plans: Wish lists formulated during "retreats" at upscale country inns, rustic conference centres, and at long lunches in downtown Ottawa or Gatineau.

Synergy: The combination of two or more elements for a greater effect. In Ottawa this means mixing a variety of objectives together with no intention of being able to measure or be responsible for their outcome.

Transparency: Refers to what is left of reports, documents and memos after the civil servants black out material.

Under advisement: Matters taken "under advisement" are generally those which do not reflect existing policies or plans, and never will.

Use it or lose it: One of the cardinal sins of government. This is a refrain heard annually in every department of every ministry at every level of government in the last quarter of the fiscal year. If budgeted money isn't spent in the year for which it was approved, it goes back to the general pot. Worse, bureaucrats can't get it back in the next year.

Utilize: Pretentious way to say "use." To utilize suggests a more efficient way of using resources.

Vision: Very common Ottawa term, pilfered from the private sector. Most common Ottawa vision is of shifting landscapes.

Whistle blower: Someone who lends out his civil service decoder ring to a media person.

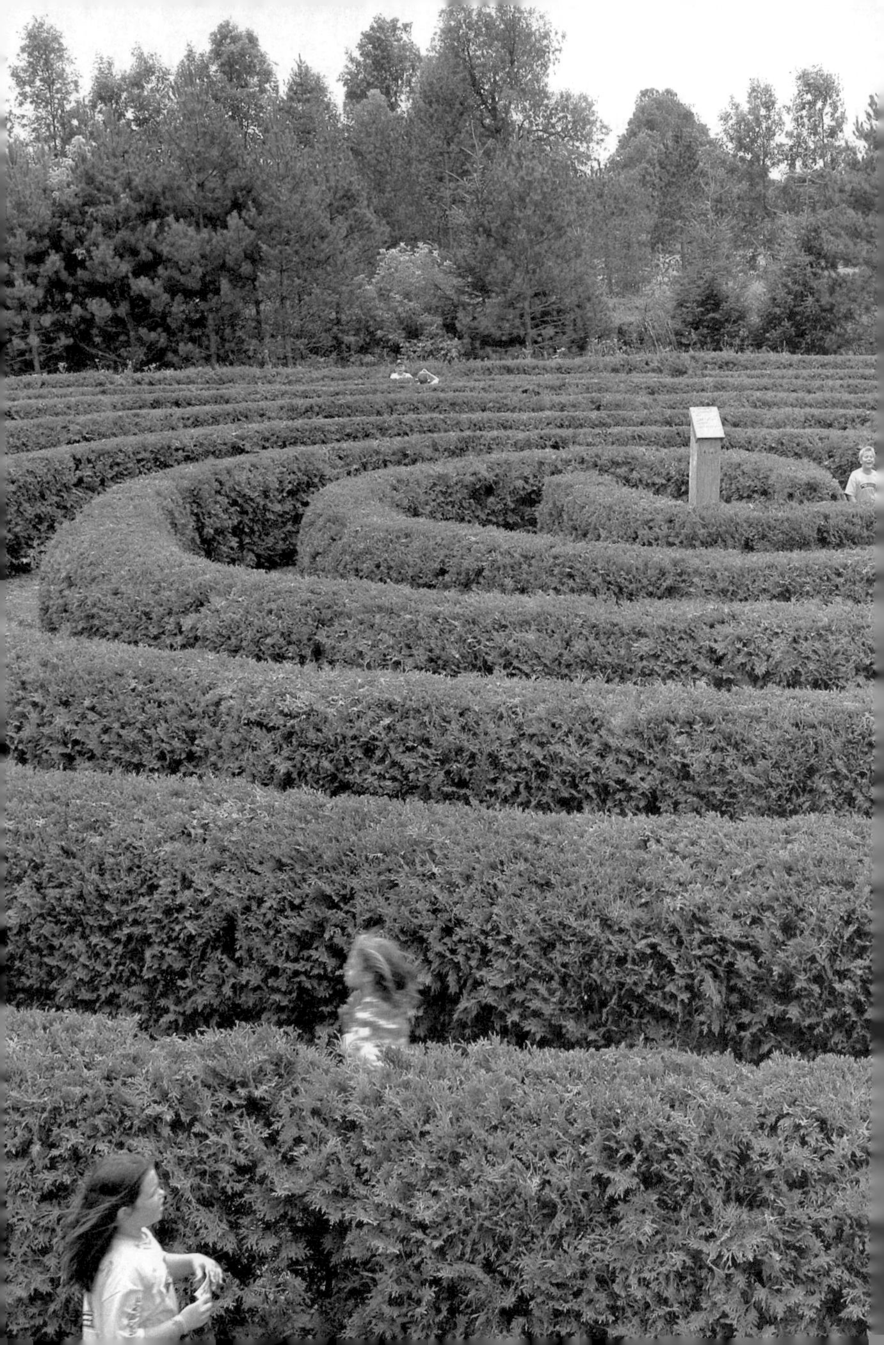

URBAN GEOGRAPHY

Urban Geography

Around 13,000 years ago, had the city of Ottawa existed, its denizens would have been trying to figure out how to live under a kilometre of ice. Luckily, that was the last of the four major ice ages, and Ottawa's share—the Wisconsin Glacier—was thawing about then. Unfortunately, the water resulting from the great thaw was slow in retreating. As a result, the area was submerged under Lake Iroquois at about the 12,000-year mark.

As the glacier continued its retreat, Lake Iroquois went along with it. The glacier gouged a channel deep enough to allow the Atlantic Ocean to surge in, creating the Champlain Sea.

As the Champlain Sea retreated, rock, then shrub-like vegetation, and, finally, great forests emerged. That was 6,000 years ago. Today, some say, Ottawa's Senate Chamber harbours folks who remember those times. Be that as it may, the Ottawa region, an unlikely backwater in the Canadian wilderness, at a melding of three rivers—the Ottawa, Rideau and Gatineau—was poised for greatness.

Did you know...

. . . that the watershed of the Ottawa River is twice the size of New Brunswick and larger than Greece or England?

TODAY

Ottawa sits pretty on three rivers just south of the Gatineau Hills. Ottawa's current boundaries (established by amalgamation on January 1, 2001) encompass a municipality that is 80 percent rural. Indeed, the accessibility of the outdoors is one of the city's most defining and attractive aspects.

Ottawa encompasses an area of 2,800 square kilometres, making it just larger than Luxembourg and just smaller than Samoa. Ottawa's population is comparable to those of San Jose, California; Indianapolis, Indiana and Oslo, Norway.

The oldest section of Ottawa is not in Ottawa at all. It was on the northern banks of the Ottawa River that Philemon Wright and his fellow settlers put down their roots, in what is now Gatineau, Quebec. While these separate municipalities are located in different provinces, people flow back and forth across the river for work and play, enjoying the best of what both cities have to offer.

LATITUDE AND LONGITUDE

Ottawa is located at 45° 19'N latitude, at approximately the same latitude line as Venice, Italy; Bordeaux, France and Sapporo, Japan. The longitude of 75° 40'W, approximates the longitude of Bogota, Colombia, Kingston, Jamaica and Lima, Peru.

THREE RIVERS RUN THROUGH IT

The cities of Ottawa and Gatineau owe their existence to a river, or more precisely to three rivers. The Ottawa River rises from its source in Lake Capimitchigama in the Laurentian mountains of central Quebec, flows west to Lake Timiskaming where it reaches the Ontario border, then flows southeast to Ottawa and Gatineau where it tumbles over the Chaudière Falls and further takes in the Rideau and Gatineau rivers.

The 1,130 km Ottawa River was first used by the voyageurs as an alternate westward route, bypassing the lower St. Lawrence River and Great Lakes. Traveling Ottawa's tributaries, voyageurs could navigate

URBAN GEOGRAPHY

the river's vast 146,300 square km watershed, or they could use it to reach as far as Lakes Huron and Superior.

The Gatineau River, at 386 km, is significantly smaller than the Ottawa River, and owes its prominence to the timber industry. Every spring for decades the river was choked with logs destined for Montreal via the Ottawa River and from there to the St. Lawrence.

As part of the Rideau Canal system, the 146 km Rideau River took on short-lived military and commercial significance. The Rideau River flows north from Upper Rideau Lake and empties into the Ottawa River at Rideau Falls. The Rideau Canal, which allows travel from Ottawa to the city of Kingston on Lake Ontario, was formed by joining the Rideau River with the Cataraqui River.

The fur trade, of course, has gone and the area's timber industry diminished. The Rideau Canal has been given over to vacationers. Despite that, the Ottawa River and its watershed remain vital to the region. Because of its many dams and reservoirs, the river basin is now one of the most highly regulated fresh water catchments in Canada, providing 14 billion cubed metres of water storage.

The significance of the river to the city of Ottawa is such that it is hard to imagine one without the other. Together with the canal, it has shaped the face of the city and provided the impetus for the city's cultural vibrancy.

Did you know...

... that rafting the timber chute on the Ottawa River at the city was a thrilling attraction to Ottawa's visiting dignitaries, including royals, and that local citizens used to line the chute to cheer and wave them on?

Take 5: BARRY WELLAR'S TOP FIVE RETAIL AND RESIDENTIAL STREETS IN OTTAWA

Dr. Barry Wellar is Professor Emeritus of Geography, University of Ottawa, and is president of Wellar Consulting Inc. He is a member of the Canadian Institute of Planners, a Distinguished Research Fellow and the recipient of numerous awards in geography, transportation and information systems. He is internationally recognized for his work on pedestrians' security, walkable communities, sustainable transportation and urban development.

RETAIL

1. **The ByWard Market** is a twelve-block area of diverse building styles (including heritage) in downtown Ottawa that has high-quality restaurants, a full mix of pubs and bars, a variety of fruit and vegetable vendors and food stores, an eclectic mix of other retail establishments and a very lively walking, talking and observing environment.

2. **Richmond Road in the Village of Westboro** between Golden Avenue and Kirkwood Avenue. This little gem offers a full array of eating, drinking, browsing and buying opportunities for both locals and visitors, and is a very good place to saunter.

3. **Bank Street from Sunnyside to the Rideau River** is a curvy, slightly hilly bit of retailing activity with lots of small, fun-to-visit stores and shops.

4. **Rideau Street from Sussex Drive to Charlotte Street**, once at the top of Ottawa's retail ladder, hit bottom, and is now dealing with people problems and brutal traffic conditions. But Rideau Street is a survivor that offers a sense of history, a wide array of retail goods and services and a vibrancy that makes it a fun place for a walk-and-shop trip.

5. **Merivale Road from Baseline to Hunt Club Road** is a cheek-by-jowl big-box and shopping centre mish-mash offering every

URBAN GEOGRAPHY

good or service imaginable. It is best traversed by car, truck, SUV, or helicopter on Saturdays, and despite its architectural, landscaping, design and aesthetic shortcomings, it is a popular retail destination.

RESIDENTIAL

1. **The Glebe** is a downtown area that is under pressure from cut-through traffic, but it remains a classic residential neighbourhood with solid, older houses of mixed architectural styles, massive trees, lots of gardens, retail, community services and parks within walking distance, and lots of people out and about. It is a great residential streetscape.

2. **Sandy Hill** abuts Rideau Street to the north, the University of Ottawa to the west, and the Rideau River on the east. Housing styles, quality, density and intensity of use vary accordingly to accentuate a gently hilly streetscape that is marked by a mix of vistas, and lots of building and landscaping eye appeal for walkers, joggers and cyclists.

3. **Ottawa South and Ottawa East** are two adjoining neighborhoods situated between the Rideau River and Rideau Canal. They are extensions of the Glebe in part, and offer a variety of street patterns, diverse housing styles, a mix of lot uses, an abundance of nature and excellent gardens.

4. **The area bounded by Byron Avenue, Holland Avenue, Island Park Drive and the Queensway** is about 15 blocks of outstanding eye appeal with diverse architecture, variations in landscaping and gardening and a very nice walk to the restaurants and shops on Wellington Street.

5. **New Edinburgh is between the Rideau River and Rideau Hall**, and offers heritage buildings, diverse architectural styles, plenty of exposure to nature and short, eye-catching walks to water and public gardens. Retail is just blocks away.

GETTING 'ROUND

The city sprawls every which way out from the river and the canal. Street names can help navigation, or not. Downtown names reflect Empire, early history — Sparks, Wellington, Queen, Albert, Dalhousie and Rideau, to name a few. Spreading from there, the age of some residential areas can be identified because our wartime generals got the honours on street names. Somewhat newer areas have had to scramble for names but they also date themselves. Paul Anka Drive is one. William Shatner Avenue is another. But none of that really helps navigation.

The Queensway Almost all places accessible from west to east can be reached from this highway. This is to Ottawa what the 401 is to Toronto without the gridlock, though rush hours can still be a pain.

Hunt Club Road Another east-west artery, crossing the city's south end and providing easy access to the airport, as also does Bronson Avenue, the latter far more scenic and running from downtown past Carleton University.

Bank Street From the Parliament Buildings, through the heart of the Glebe, and all the way south to the TransCanada Highway (401), this is Ottawa's Yonge Street. Schlocky, sleazy, sensual, sophisticated, scenic — Bank Street has it all.

Ottawa River Parkway A fine east-west bypass that runs from Parliament Hill, along the Ottawa River, westward to the edge of "old Ottawa," where it hooks up with Carling Avenue to take you to Kanata's high tech core.

Rideau Street From downtown, along the edge of the ByWard Market, this street transforms into Montreal Road, which, in turn, is the path through Vanier into Ottawa's points east.

URBAN GEOGRAPHY

Take 5 — SALLY COUTTS AND STUART LAZEAR'S FIVE FAVOURITE HERITAGE STRUCTURES

Sally Coutts and Stuart Lazear are heritage planners with the city of Ottawa. Here, they tell us their favourite structures in Ottawa.

1. **Aberdeen Pavilion** (1898, Moses Edey, Architect). The last remaining 19th-century exhibition hall in Canada was constructed in two months. The original Ottawa Senators won the Stanley Cup here in 1909.

2. **Library of Parliament** (1859-77, designed by Thomas Fuller and Chilion Jones; recently restored). The only part of the Centre Block to escape the fire of 1916, this excellent example of Gothic Revival architecture is well suited to its prominent location above the cliffs of Parliament Hill.

3. **Bank of Montreal**, 144 Wellington Street (1930-34, Ernest Barott, Architect). This building features an allegorical relief sculpture by Emil Sieburn celebrating Canadian industry and commerce.

4. **Minto Bridges** (1900-02). Named for the eighth Governor-General, the Earl of Minto, this is part of an early ceremonial route from Rideau Hall to Parliament, and was one of the first projects of the Ottawa Improvement Commission (precursor of the NCC). Built by the city of Ottawa under the direction of Robert Surtees, City Engineer.

5. **St. Clare's Roman Catholic Church**, 4009 Dwyer Hill Road (1915, Francis Sullivan, Architect). This is one of two churches designed by Sullivan, an early Canadian follower of American architect Frank Lloyd Wright. The steeply pitched bell-cast roof, flared overhanging eaves, pagoda-topped bell tower, and the use of stucco with strong horizontal wooden accents illustrate the influence of Wright's Prairie Style.

Did you know...

...that Ottawa produces 338 million litres of drinking water each day?

GOING GREEN

The Greenbelt is a 20,350 hectare band of open lands and forests surrounding the nation's capital on the Ontario side of the Ottawa River. It was first proposed in 1950 by French planner Jacques Gréber as part of a strategy to create a beautiful and distinctive setting for the capital. The Greenbelt was intended to protect the rural land bordering the Capital from the haphazard urban sprawl.

Acting on Gréber's plan, the federal government began acquiring land in 1956. Today, the Greenbelt encircles the Capital from Shirley's Bay on the west to Green's Creek on the east. Most of the total area, or 14,950 hectares, is owned and managed by the National Capital Commission. The rest is held by other federal departments and private interests.

URBAN OASIS

The City of Ottawa maintains more than 10,000 hectares of forests in five municipal conservation forests and several protected environmental areas, including the South March Highlands and Marlborough Forest. The city also maintains 200,000 street trees.

Did you know...

...that Ottawa invests more than $2 million annually to maintain and replace park infrastructure such as play structures?

Did you know...

...that at one time the Ottawa River was connected via the Mattawa River to Lakes Superior and Huron?

URBAN GEOGRAPHY

Take 5 FIVE FREE THINGS TO DO IN OTTAWA

1. The air we breathe is free, so far. Also free—if one looks to the dawn and dusk skies of Ottawa in spring and fall—is the awesome appearance of hundreds of **Canada geese** in V-formation overhead. Ottawa is a natural migratory flyway for the big birds. You'll hear them honking before you see them. Still, if you miss them in the sky, head over to the Central Experimental Farm where the flocks like to feed, carpeting entire fields when they do so.

2. When the **House of Commons** is in session, the visitors' gallery is open on a first come, first serve basis. To ensure a seat, contact your MP ahead of time—MP's take pleasure in accommodating non-issue interests of their constituents. Best time to attend: Question Period. That's when they play for the cameras.

3. For pomp and ceremony, the daily **Changing of the Guard** on Parliament Hill is a delight, as is a quick trip to the stables of the RCMP Musical Ride where, with luck, the horses can be seen going through their routine. Make sure to come between the first of June and the end of August.

4. Glitz, glamour, the rattle of dice, whirr of roulette wheels, clatter and jangle of slot machines are all free at the **Casino du Lac Leamy** in Gatineau. Playing is, of course, not so free. Every year the casino also holds an International Fireworks Competition that lights up both sides of the river.

5. **Little Ray's Reptile Zoo** is Canada's best of its kind and it charges admission. But in early spring, pull on gumboots, grab a powerful flashlight and a camera. For free you can accompany Little Ray himself on a nighttime hike into a swamp to check out frogs and other creatures when they come out of the mud to breed. Or, he'll take you slogging into a river still choked with ice to observe eastern Ontario's foremost mud puppy breeding ground. He'll even tell you why it's important for you to be out there freezing. The best part, he's so charismatic, you'll believe him.

OTTAWA BOASTS
- 2,023 km of local/residential roads
- 1,402 km of major collector roads
- 1,150 km of minor collector roads
- 936 km of arterial roads
- 97 km of transit/freeways
- 5,600 km of roadways
- 5,000 km of paved roads
- 600 km of gravel roads
- 475 roadway bridges
- 1,580 km of sidewalks
- 65 km of transitway
- 850 parks
- 2,853 hectares of parkland
- 6,648 hectares of natural parkland
- 9,501 hectares of open space
- 2 city-owned stadiums (TD Place Stadium — capacity 28,826/ Lynx Stadium — capacity 10,332)
- 1 privately owned major stadium (Canadian Tire Centre, home of the Ottawa Senators, capacity 19,153)
- 119 community centres
- 4 senior centres

UP THERE
- Rank of Ottawa among the top cities worldwide in terms of health and cleanliness, according to a study conducted by Mercer Human Resource Consulting which measured the quality and availability of hospital and medical supplies and levels of air pollution and infectious diseases in 215 cities: 4
- Rank of Ottawa in Mercer's broader "quality of life" survey: 18

URBAN GEOGRAPHY

Lake 5 FIVE OTTAWA AREA PARKS

1. **Gatineau Park:** The 19th century timber barons spared this area, the National Capital Commission snatched up ownership, and the park now stands as a vast unspoiled testament to what drew our forebears to this region and what keeps us here. Add to that, the Gatineau Hills which are visible from almost everywhere in Ottawa across the river.

2. **MacKenzie King Estate:** This historic parkland is more than a preservation of the summer home of one of Canada's most influential Prime Ministers. It borders on Kingsmere Lake, provides hands-on access to King's summer house, boathouse and his facsimile Graeco-Roman ruins. If that's not enough, High Tea is served daily in the comfort to be expected of any Victorian occasion.

3. **Aboretum:** This is the centrepiece of the Experimental Farm, yet it's tucked away from the barns, greenhouses and fields of the farm proper. Landscaped grounds, trees otherwise native only to other parts of the world, folks fishing along the Dow's Lake shore, a constant chorus of bullfrogs in counterpoint to joyous barking of unleashed dogs – one of the few parks in Ottawa where dogs can go unleashed, albeit supervised by their owners.

4. **Hampton Park:** Timelessly caught old stately homes, including embassy residences and the gritty reality of a cut-rate supermarket, this neighborhood park is an Ottawa treasure. On one end are ball diamonds, play structures and a swimming pool, buttressing the Queensway. The rest of the park is bush, hills and even a wee creek for those adventurous enough to trace its meanderings off-trail.

5. **Papanack Zoo and Park:** This privately-owned facility on the outskirts of Ottawa has been one family's labour of love for many years. The park is a full-day excursion, animals on hand ranging from a pride of lions to snow leopards, monkeys everywhere, and, of course, a petting area. In back of the park, not be missed, is just about the ugliest tom turkey ever to escape the dinner table. This is as close as Ottawa comes to a city zoo. Correction: This is the city zoo!

53

RIDEAU CANAL BY THE NUMBERS
- Year built: 1832
- Entire length: 202 km
- Man-made length: 19 km
- Number of locks: 47
- Number of stations: 24
- Final Cost: $1.76 million

RIDEAU CANAL SKATEWAY
- Year first officially opened to skaters: 1971
- Skating length: 7.8 km
- Ice surface size: 165,621 m^2
- Approximate number of skaters: 1 million yearly, 19,000 daily
- Heated chalets: 6
- Skate rental/sharpening/boot checks: 3
- Parking lots: 6
- Washrooms: 5

Source: the NCC.

BIKING COUNTRY
- The Capital Pathway network is one of the continent's largest networks of cycling pathways at 600kms, linking natural areas, parks, gardens, museums and attractions.
- Alcatel-Lucent Sunday Bikedays ensure over 50 km of parkways are closed to motor vehicle traffic every Sunday morning all summer long.
- Mountain biking is permitted in Gatineau Park all summer but be sure to mind the rules — conservation officers patrol the area and are authorized to hand out fines for infractions.

Source: the NCC.

Did you know...

. . . that the Rideau Canal was designated the 'World's Largest Naturally Frozen Ice Rink' by the *Guinness Book of World Records*?

URBAN GEOGRAPHY

DOWNTOWN
- Number of people who live downtown: 99,500
- Percentage of Ottawa's population that lives downtown: 10.9
- Number of housing units: 48,735
- Percentage of Ottawa's housing units that are downtown: 14
- Number of apartment rental units downtown: 8,784
- Average apartment rental: $1,377.00/monthly
- Number of condos downtown: 1,689 (50 percent of Ottawa's condos)
- Percentage of Ottawa's retail space which is downtown: 16
- Percentage of Ottawa's retail outlets that are downtown: 26
- Number of museums downtown: 15

Source: City of Ottawa.

THE PARLIAMENT BUILDINGS

Ottawa is home to the ultimate heritage buildings: Parliament. Construction began in 1860, and five years later, civil servants began moving into the not-quite-completed buildings. In 1867, the Library opened, and the legislative chamber was enlarged.

In 1916, only the Library survived a fire that demolished the rest of the Centre Block. It was then rebuilt in the Gothic Revival style. The East and West Blocks were designed in the Civil Gothic style. Sandstone was used throughout, with elaborate decorative carving. The Mackenzie Tower of the West Block was the tallest structure in Ottawa until the Peace Tower (90 m high) was completed in 1927.

HOTEL TO THE HILL

Five long years had passed between turning of the first sod for the Fairmont Château Laurier and its official opening in 1912. The opening was a signal moment for the young city. Elegance and refinement had finally come to rough and tumble Ottawa.

The Château was built in the French Renaissance style, the interior graced with marble floors, gleaming brass, high ceilings, thick wool carpets and furniture selected to integrate with and accent the struc-

Did you know...

...that the city collects approximately 62,820 tonnes of blue and black box items for recycling annually. This results in $8,031,000 of revenue.

ture — rich but not opulent, stately rather than garish.

The exterior faces the city, the river and Parliament Hill. The facade is granite and limestone, its roof copper, its majesty as one of the finest of its era's railway hotels unquestioned. Immediately the Château became a home away from home for the country's politicians. Its dining, tea rooms and lounges, corridors and suites became stomping grounds for deal-makers, dignitaries, the rich and famous and the royal.

None of this has changed much. The Château has aged with dignity, and still remains very much at the hub of Ottawa and one of the most important fixtures on the Ottawa skyline.

GET ON BOARD THE O-TRAIN

Ottawa's O-Train uses an 8 km stretch of existing railway and is the first single operator passenger rail service on the continent. It was launched on October 15, 2001 and:

- Includes five stations (Bayview, Carling, Carleton University, Confederation Heights and Greenboro)
- Has room for 135 seated and 150 standing passengers
- Is used by up to 10,300 passengers daily, 2.4 million yearly
- Can reach top speeds of 120 km/hr
- Weighs 72,000 kg
- Has six trains

A second line, the Confederation Line, is set to open in 2018.

Did you know...

...that Ottawa's public transit offers Rack & Roll service on 300 buses, allowing commuters to travel with their bikes?

URBAN GEOGRAPHY

RIDIN' THE BUS

The Transitway is a huge part of Ottawa's bus system, providing fast service across the whole city and regularly intersects with the O-Train. The Transitway:

- Covers an area of 413 km^2
- Has an average daily ridership of approximately 220,000
- Has about 2,200 employees
- Has 6,290 bus stops
- Has 30kms of bus only lanes

TRANSIT FARES

- Monthly pass, regular adult: $113.75
- Monthly pass, rural adult: $130
- Monthly pass, senior: $43.25
- Monthly pass, regular student: $89.75
- Children 5 and under: free
- Day pass: $10.25
- Tickets, adult: $3.40 each
- O-Train tickets: $3.35 each

Source: the OC Transpo.

PLAY IT AGAIN!

Ottawa has many sporting venues, events and players, all managed by the city's sports field operation team. The city offers its sports nuts:

- 21 indoor swimming pools
- 9 outdoor swimming pools
- 58 wading pools
- 5 city-operated beaches
- 74 splash spray pads
- 34 city-operated arenas
- 305 sports fields
- 250 outdoor rinks
- 331 separate ice surfaces

- 1 city-owned golf course
- 27 public golf courses (Ottawa-Gatineau)
- 300 tennis courts (172 lighted) in 108 facilities
- 13 skateboard parks

STANDING HISTORY
3,500 of Ottawa's homes and buildings are designated heritage structures—330 of them individually, and 3,200 within the boundaries of a heritage conservation district.

A GLOBAL VILLAGE
International embassies and commissions are scattered throughout Ottawa. More than 130 countries and bodies (including entities like the Arctic Council, the European Union and the International Joint Commission) inhabit properties, elaborate or modest, in the heart of downtown or on sleepy residential streets. A certain flavour is imparted to life in the capital when you can find yourself living beside, say, the Malawi High Commission or the Embassy of Vietnam.

Source: Ottawa Kiosk.

LIVING HISTORY: THE CENTRAL EXPERIMENTAL FARM
Ottawa's rural character was ingrained in its heart when the Central Experimental Farm was established in 1886 as the central research station for the Department of Agriculture (now Agriculture and Agri-Food Canada). Here, the farm's first director, William Saunders, planted the first 20 trees of the 63-acre Arboretum in 1889. Saunders and his two sons developed Marquis, the early-maturing wheat that became one of Canada's great exports.

Research is the primary pursuit on the 400 plus hectare National Historic Site, but also welcomes visitors. The attractions that this 19th century landscape offer include the Arboretum (2,400 varieties of trees and shrubs), working barns and greenhouses, wildlife and ornamental gardens, the Agriculture Museum and several heritage buildings.

URBAN GEOGRAPHY

Did you know...

...that within the first three days of completion, the Rideau Canal Pedestrian Bridge linking Centretown to Sandy Hill was used by almost 5,000 cyclists, rollerbladers and pedestrians?

CORNY SOLUTION

Along Ottawa's rural roads, cornstalks double as snow breaks in the winter. The city pays farmers not to cut the stalks down with the late fall harvest, thus saving the expense of purchasing, erecting, disassembling and storing seasonal fencing. This natural barrier is particularly effective along north-south routes, because snow blows most often from west to east.

PROJECT PORCHLIGHT

Ottawa South became a campaign partner in Project Porchlight, which saw over 300 volunteers deliver more than 16,000 energy-saving compact fluorescent light bulbs door-to-door as part of its pilot project. Consumers redeemed more than 9,000 coupons for these bulbs at Giant Tiger. The city worked closely with Hydro Ottawa on a strategy to expand Project Porchlight across all of Ottawa and:

- Worked with dozens of communities and 53,000 participants to undertake 750 cleanup projects as part of the Spring Cleaning the Capital challenge to help keep Ottawa clean, green and litter-free.
- Constructed the downtown-to-Barrhaven O-Train, which began operation starting in spring 2010. The expanded O-Train delivered many benefits to Ottawa, including reduced traffic congestion on roads and virtually no emissions for cleaner air.

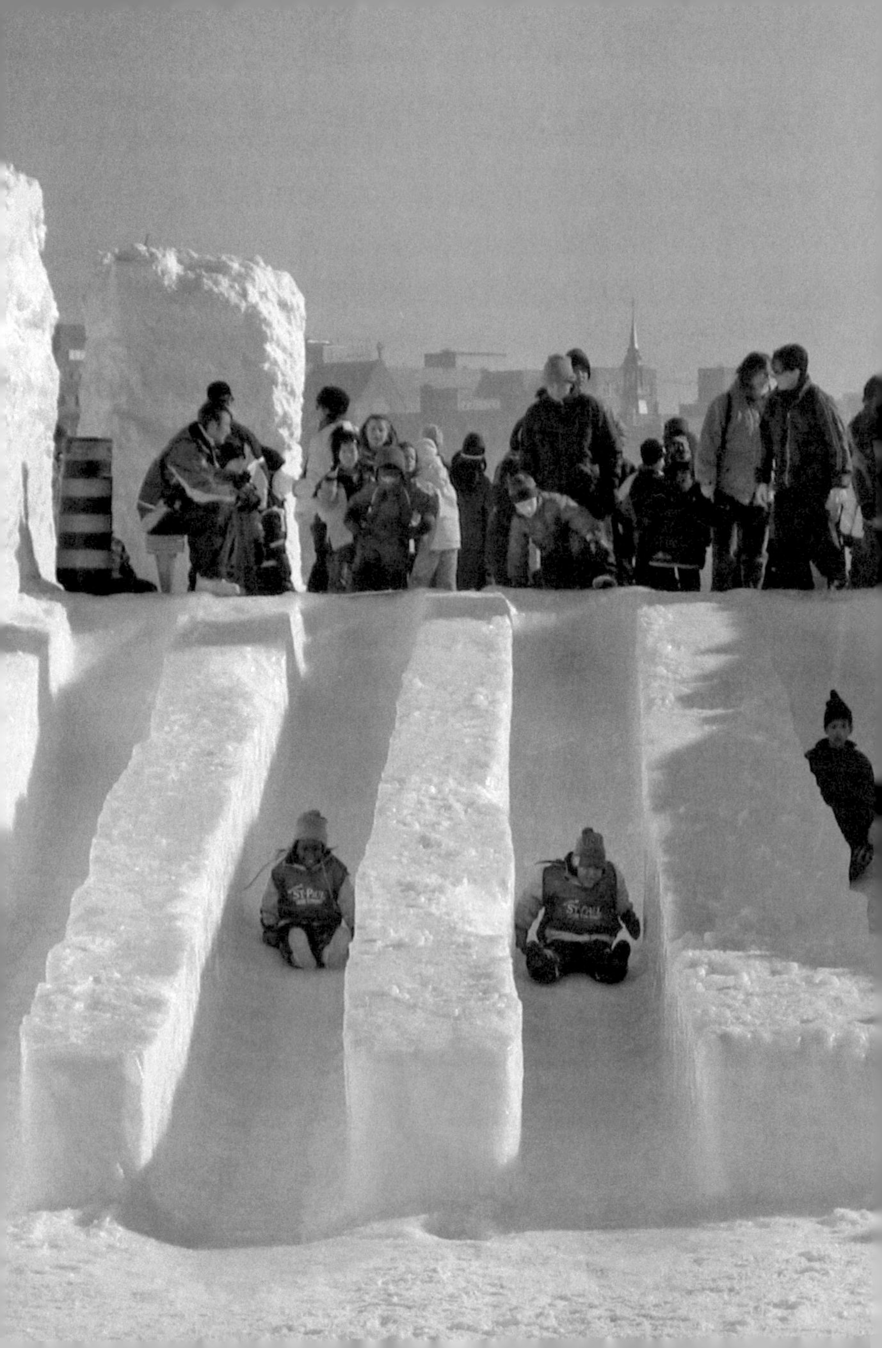
ST-PAUL
ST-PAUL

Weather and Climate

Ottawa is a city that experiences four very distinct seasons. Because it is Canada, some seasons (dare we say winter) are longer than others. Its distance from any of Canada's oceans means the climate is continental, with occasional forays of a maritime climate.

The lack of a large body of water nearby means the moderating influence of the ocean on temperature is absent. Cloud cover, which generally shades and insulates, is also reduced and precipitation is diminished. As a result, temperatures can and do vary widely. Mark Twain's suggestion to wait ten minutes could quite easily apply to Ottawa. During the course of a year, Ottawa endures extremes from -36°C to 37°C.

Incursions of maritime climate bring with them turbulent systems and changing weather. The frontal zone that separates the maritime climate and the dominant, dryer continental climate frequently cross the area.

The weather can also vary across the city. The urban heat-island effect raises temperatures in the centre of the built-up area. (The principal weather station is on the cooler, southern outskirts, at the airport). Precipitation tends to be lighter towards the south because of the topographical influence of the escarpment north of the city. Numerous rivers also have local effects.

MONTHLY AVERAGE TEMPERATURES (°C)

MAX

Jan	Feb	Mar	Apr	May	Jun	Jul	Aug	Sep	Oct	Nov	Dec
-5	-4	2	11	19	24	26	25	20	13	5	-3

MIN

Jan	Feb	Mar	Apr	May	Jun	Jul	Aug	Sep	Oct	Nov	Dec
-15	-13	-6	0	7	12	15	14	9	3	-2	-11

AND THE WINNER IS . . .

- Record High: 38°C on August 11, 1944
- Record Humidex: 46°C on July 1, 1955
- Record Rainfall (in a day): 80 mm on September 9, 1942
- Record Low: -38.9°C on December 29, 1933
- Record Snowfall (in a day): 55.9cm on January 29, 1894
- Record Wind Speed (maximum hourly speed km/h): 80 km on October 15, 1954
- Record Wind Gust: 135 km on May 11, 1959
- Record Wind Chill: -48 C on January 8, 1968

Source: Environment Canada.

HIGH TEMPS

June, July and August are the warmest months in Ottawa, having a 20°C average. Daily highs and lows generally swing about 5°C to either side of this. Although July is hottest, it beats August by only a nose, and June is not far behind. Each month can be counted on to offer several days over 30°C: July's average of five days doubles that in each of the other two months.

Ottawa is only 2°C from the pinnacle of the hottest summer: Kamloops, B.C. has the highest average afternoon temperature at 27°C.

Source: Environment Canada.

WEATHER

Take 5 IAN BLACK'S TOP FIVE SEVERE OTTAWA WEATHER EVENTS

Ian Black is a long-time CBC weather forecaster in Ottawa and the first person ever endorsed by the Canadian Meteorological and Oceanographic Society. He is a graduate of the University of Waterloo and has earned a certificate in Weathercasting.

1. **The 1998 Ice Storm:** In January 1998, much of eastern Ontario and southern Quebec, and portions of the Maritimes and northern New England were encased in ice after five days of freezing rain. Power outages were commonplace (in some cases for weeks), and eventually the army was called in to help out with one of the costliest storms ever recorded.

2. **The snowy winter of 1971-72:** More than 400 cm of snow fell in the "white winter," which challenged even the hardiest of Ottawans. The white stuff started in November and never really let up for long. This winter is the reason why most Ottawa adults think the snow banks seemed higher as a kid — they were!

3. **Hurricane Frances, September 9, 2004:** Everyone in Ottawa has seen rainstorms before, but few like the deluge of that late-summer day. 136 mm of rain fell as what was left of a major hurricane roared through eastern Ontario and western Quebec. The entire month normally brings 85 mm of rain.

4. **The Aylmer Tornado:** At 3 pm on August 4, 1994, a vicious F3 tornado ripped through a large chunk of Aylmer, Quebec, across the river from Ottawa. Damage was severe, but miraculously no one was killed. It serves as a reminder that twisters are not just a worry for residents of Kansas and Tornado Alley.

5. **Climate change:** Anyone who lives in Ottawa long enough will experience almost anything, from dry spells (22 days is the record), to severe cold snaps and heat waves, to intense wet spells. It seems, however, that as the climate changes, we will see even stranger weather events. During the winter of 2006–07, for example, there was no snow cover until the second half of January! People were riding bikes instead of skating on the canal.

ON THE SUNNY SIDE

The sun shines on Ottawa on 303 days in an average year. June has the least amount of cloud on average. November earns its gloomy reputation, being the cloudiest month, but December is almost equal. Ottawans have an average of 2,061 hours of sun per year. Medicine Hat, AB, has the most sunny hours with 2,513, while Calgary has sun on the most days with 333.

Source: Environment Canada.

Winterlude

If you live in a country where winter is your longest season, you better find ways to enjoy it. If you are smart, you've made winter your friend. On three weekends in February, Ottawa does just that. Winterlude is a festival that celebrates outdoor winter recreation and entertainment, and to the surprise of many, it has become an international tourism hit.

Winterlude's beginnings can be traced back to January of 1971 when a 5 km-long section of the Rideau Canal in downtown Ottawa was first opened for skating. Although it would be another eight years before Winterlude became an official winter festival, it is the Rideau Canal Skateway that was its inspiration and remains its centrepiece. The skateway is the largest naturally frozen ice rink in the world. It is 7.8 km long and larger than 90 Olympic-sized hockey rinks. It usually opens at the end of December. In 2014-15, more than 900,000 people visited Ottawa during Winterlude, generating more than $80 million for the city.

The crowd favourite during Winterlude is the snow park in Gatineau, primarily because of its slides and sculptures. Ice sculptures are works of art in their own right.

Winterlude is a reminder of what pleasures there are to be had outdoors during winter. The fact that visitors come from all over the world to celebrate with Ottawans has surprised the local population. Skating, snow sculptures, heated change rooms, huts selling "beavertails" and hot chocolate, and special performances have done the most improbable of things. It has turned winter into a star.

WEATHER

Take 5 FIVE WEATHER-DEPENDANT FUN ACTIVITIES

1. **Skating the Rideau Canal**. Most years, the 7.8 km-long skateway opens sometime after New Year's Day. It takes 10 to 14 consecutive days of -20°C to -15°C for the ice surface to attain the minimum safe thickness of 25-30 cm.

2. **Making maple syrup**. Ottawa's Vanier quarter boasts the only sugar bush within city limits in North America. Ideal conditions for the best sap run: nights below -4°C, followed by days with maximums between 4°C and 8°C.

3. **Hot-air ballooning**. Huge, colourful orbs floating along like low clouds are a frequent sight in all seasons as long as it's not snowing or raining. The preferred northerly winds take the balloons across downtown Ottawa to safe landing sites on the outskirts. Light winds are ideal: up to 10 km/h for take-off, up to 15 km/h for landing, and up to 30 km/h aloft. Most capitals prohibit ballooning in their airspace.

4. **Urban ice fishing**. The hopeful try their luck less than 1.5 km downriver from Parliament Hill. Ice on the Ottawa River must be at least 10 cm thick to support a person's weight.

5. **Paragliding off the escarpment**. Those nervy enough to leap from the Champlain Lookout in Gatineau Park look for west or southwest winds of 5 km/h to 15 km/h (and no precipitation) before they consider floating the 300 m to the ground. (Gatineau Park may be beyond the Ottawa River in Quebec, but this wilderness is part of the heart and soul of Ottawans nonetheless).

They Said It

> "At home til 3, then to the Dept with my husband and then to drive with him across the ice, such smooth sleighing; the whole country is a sheet of unbroken snow, dazzling to look upon; the air is rare with cold; the lightness of the atmosphere quite remarkable."
> – Agnes Macdonald, wife of Prime Minister John A. Macdonald, writing in her diary in 1868, on his 53rd birthday

PRECIPITATION

Ottawa rarely suffers long wet or dry periods. It rains or snows on at least a third of the days each month, averaging 40 percent for the year. In March and November it rains about as often as it snows.

Yearly average precipitation of 944 mm places Ottawa in about the middle of the pack in the wettest city ranking (which includes both rain and snow). The winner of this soggy honour is Prince Rupert, B.C., which endures 2,594 mm of precipitation in a year. The national average is 522 mm.

IT'S RAINING, IT'S POURING

When it rains in Ottawa, it rains cats and dogs. The annual 732 mm that falls is well above the Canadian average of 345 mm. All this falls on only about 115 days, while the much smaller national average is spread out over 145 days. Umbrellas are raised overhead in every month. July gets the most rain with 90.6 mm, although May has the most rainy days with 13.

Did you know...

... that in 1992 someone tried to get Ottawa radio station CFMO formally disciplined by the Canada Broadcast Standards Council for broadcasting weather forecasts that did not come true? The complainant lost.

WEATHER

Ice Storm of 1998

The Ice Storm of 1998 was a beautiful disaster. Six days of freezing rain in January turned a vast area of eastern Canada (from Georgian Bay to the Bay of Fundy) into an awe-inspiring, crystalline wonderland. The weight of all that picturesque ice, however, brought down power lines, poles and pylons. Eventually, about 700,000 persons in eastern Ontario alone were without electricity.

The trouble started when a warm, wet air mass became trapped between two cold air masses, keeping conditions in place for days. Raindrops formed in the warm air, while the cold air layer below was too thin to freeze the drops into snow or ice pellets. Instead the drops froze almost immediately upon impact, forming a smooth layer of ice.

In Ottawa, 70 mm of freezing rain fell in less than six days; an average January delivers 70 mm of rain and snow. Total precipitation during those six days reached 85 mm. From January 4 to 9, freezing rain fell for 63 hours and 42 minutes. In an average year, Ottawa gets 64 hours of freezing rain, spread over 17 days.

Including Ottawa, ten of 11 municipalities within the (former) Regional Municipality of Ottawa-Carleton called a state of emergency. Inhabitants hunkered down at home, with friends and neighbours, and in shelters to wait for the power (and heat) to come back on, and for the treacherous ice on sidewalks, roads and buildings to be melted, removed, or covered with snow.

The end of the freezing rain was not the end of the trouble. In the next week, it got a lot colder, with lows often in the -20°C to -16°C range. Another 11 cm of snow fell. The conditions made outdoor work more challenging for the clean-up and repair crews. Shelters counted 1,007 overnight stays from January 9 to 18. Eventually, the weather eased up, and that winter turned out to be the second-mildest on record.

Ottawa never lost its electricity supply completely. Rural areas were hit much harder. Some customers were without electricity for hours, others for days, and a few for as long as three weeks. Elsewhere in the storm's path, the longest wait was 33 days. Overall, one-fifth of the country's population lost power.

At least 6 million persons were affected in some way. Tragically, 35 died from causes attributable to the storm. Economically, the $3-billion cost of the damage makes it the most expensive natural disaster in Canada's history. It was the ice storm of the century.

Take 5 TOP FIVE HOTTEST DAYS IN OTTAWA'S HISTORY (FROM 1889)

1. **August 14, 1944:** 37.8 °C
2. **August 9, 2001:** 37.2 °C
3. **August 1, 1955:** 37.2 °C
4. **August 11, 1944:** 37.2 °C
5. **July 22, 1955:** 36.7 °C

Source: Environment Canada.

FREEZING RAIN

Freezing rain makes Ottawa streets and sidewalks treacherous on 17 days in typical years. This is not half as bad as they have it in Gander, NL, which usually has the most days with 39.

Source: Environment Canada.

SNOW

Ottawa's annual 236 cm of snow accounts for only 25 percent of the annual precipitation. It usually snows the most in December — 57 cm is average — but a typical winter month records 47 cm.

The white stuff sticks around — despite the fact that it snows on only 66 days annually — more than a third of the year. For 122 days, Ottawa has some snow on the ground. Average winter snow depth is 27 cm. In March 1993, people were grumbling a lot more than usual (and with good reason) about shoveling when the depth reached 135 cm.

Source: Environment Canada.

Did you know...

... that Ultimate Frisbee is played outdoors from mid-May to Halloween in all weather except lightning storms? Ottawa has the biggest Ultimate league in the world.

WEATHER

Take 5 TOP FIVE COLDEST DAYS IN OTTAWA'S HISTORY (FROM 1889)

1. **December 29, 1933:** -38.9 °C
2. **December 30, 1933:** -38.3 °C
3. **February 17, 1934:** -38.3 °C
4. **January 19, 1925:** -37.8 °C
5. **February 15, 1943:** -37.8 °C

Source: Environment Canada.

THUNDER AND LIGHTNING

A combination of climate and geography gives Ottawa more than a median share of thunderstorms and lightning. On average, the city has 24 thunderstorm days per year. Windsor, Ontario, has the most with 33 days.

Lightning tends to occur at the outer limits of elevated areas. The Ottawa Valley's proximity to the hills that surround the Ottawa River is one of the factors that contributes to the higher frequency of lightning there than in surrounding areas. Ottawa experiences a relatively high average of 90 lightning flashes a year per 100 square km. Windsor, by comparison, experiences 251 flashes.

The high frequency of lightning flashes seems to correlate with the extraordinary number of persons struck in recent years. In 2006, a man survived a strike in Ottawa. In this century already, two persons have been killed in the area. Across the Ottawa River in Quebec, a man was killed in 2007 in Gatineau, and a teenage boy was killed in 2012 near Rockland. Each year in Canada, lightning kills 6 to 12 people.

Sources: Meteorological Services Canada; Ottawa Citizen; 580 CFRA; Environment Canada.

Did you know...

. . . that of all the major capitals in the world, Ottawa holds the distinction of being the coldest and snowiest?

They Said It

> "In January 1887, I brought my Russian skis to Ottawa, the very first pair that had ever been seen in the New World. I coasted down hills on them amidst universal jeers; everyone declared they were quite unsuitable to the Canadian conditions."
> – **Lord Frederick Hamilton, brother-in-law to Governor General Lansdowne, on the sport known then as skilöbning**

FOG

Ottawa doesn't get very much fog, but when it comes, it sure can look pretty drifting over the rivers and thickening the "atmosphere" around the older buildings. Such foggy photo opportunities occur on an average of 34 days in a year. Canada's foggiest city, St. John's, NL, steals the show with 119 days.

GROWING SEASON

As in the rest of eastern Ontario, the growing season in Ottawa has been lengthening over the past 40 years. In an average year, Ottawa's gardeners can count on 120 frost-free days. Since 2000, the last spring frost has been around May 8, and the first autumn frost around October 8. In 2005, the autumn frost was one of the latest ever recorded in Ottawa, on October 20. The frost-free period that year was 161 days.

Sources: Canadian Organic Growers; Missisippi Valley Field Naturalists.

WEATHER

Take 5 TOP FIVE HEAVIEST SNOWFALLS IN A SINGLE DAY IN OTTAWA'S HISTORY (FROM 1889)

1. January 29, 1894: 55.9 cm
2. November 25, 1912: 54.1 cm
3. March 2, 1947: 48.3 cm
4. February 8, 1995: 45.7 cm
5. February 18, 2016: 50 cm

Source: Environment Canada.

DROUGHT

Record-breaking drought struck the country so hard in 2001 and 2002 that drought conditions were worse by the second year than during the 1930s dust bowl. In Ottawa, 2001 was the dryer of the two years. Only 84 percent of the annual precipitation fell that year. That July, only 43 percent of the average July rainfall was recorded. On August 14, the Ottawa River—the second-longest in Ontario—shrank to within 11 cm of its lowest level since 1951.

WIND

Ottawa is a middling windy city. Light winds of at least 5 km/h blow on an average of 249 days per year. Overall, the average speed is 13 km/h. The windiest city, St. John's, NL, blows Ottawa away with a 23 km/h average.

Tornadoes are extremely rare in the area. The closest one to Ottawa struck just on the other side of the Ottawa River in Aylmer (now Gatineau), Quebec, on August 4, 1994. Varying estimates say the winds of this F3 twister were in the 150 km/h to 200 km/h range.

Sources: National Research Council Canada; Environment Canada.

They Said It

"Our street is fearfully dangerous being covered with glare ice. This proves the law that water always freezes with the slippery side up".
– Deputy minister (1873–79) Edmund Meredith, complaining in 1877 to his diary about his neighbours' neglect of their sidewalks.

WHEN IT FEELS WORSE THAN IT IS

The colder months are the windier months in Ottawa, and most of the strongest winds (faster than 52 km/h) blow then. Wind chill becomes a daily topic of conversation and a standard item in forecasts. Typically, the wind will make it feel colder than -20°C on 52 days in a year, and 14 of these colder than -30°C.

It has never seemed colder than on January 8, 1968, when the wind chill made it feel like -48°C. *The worst it's ever been in Canada was -66°C, which earned the folks in Iqualuit the unfortunate bragging rights.*

Temperatures at the other end of the comfort range also get a boost in the warmer months, when the humidity makes the heat even more unpleasant. In July, there are 15 days on average in which humidity makes it feel hotter than 30°C, and at least one day that makes it feel at least 40°C. A 46°C humidex on July 1, 1955 is the highest ever recorded in Ottawa.

Source: Environment Canada

WEATHER

LOW TEMPS

Despite Ottawa's reputation for cold, the temperature does commonly register close to and even above freezing in winter. Nevertheless, on most days (an average of 20 per month) the mercury drops below -10°C. Almost a third of January's days will see lows below -20°C.

The unofficial winter month, December, is comparable to February, but a little bit warmer. January and February have each recorded the extreme of -36°C — both, coincidentally, on the 15th (1957 and 1943, respectively). Ottawa is around the middle of the coldest-winter continuum (which ranks the lowest average night-time temperature in December, January and February). Yellowknife, NWT, holds down one end with -29°C, and Victoria, BC, anchors the other with 1°C.

Source: Environment Canada.

WHITE CHRISTMAS

Odds are good that Ottawa will have a white Christmas. Ottawans have an 83 percent chance of realizing Bing Crosby's White Christmas dream of seeing at least two centimetres of snow on the ground on December 25. Compare this to Toronto's 57 percent likelihood, Montreal's 80 percent odds, Vancouver's 11 percent odds and Whitehorse's 100 percent chance of having a white Christmas. Ottawa recorded its record-setting Christmas Day snowfall in 1978 with 20 cm.

Source: Meteorological Services Canada.

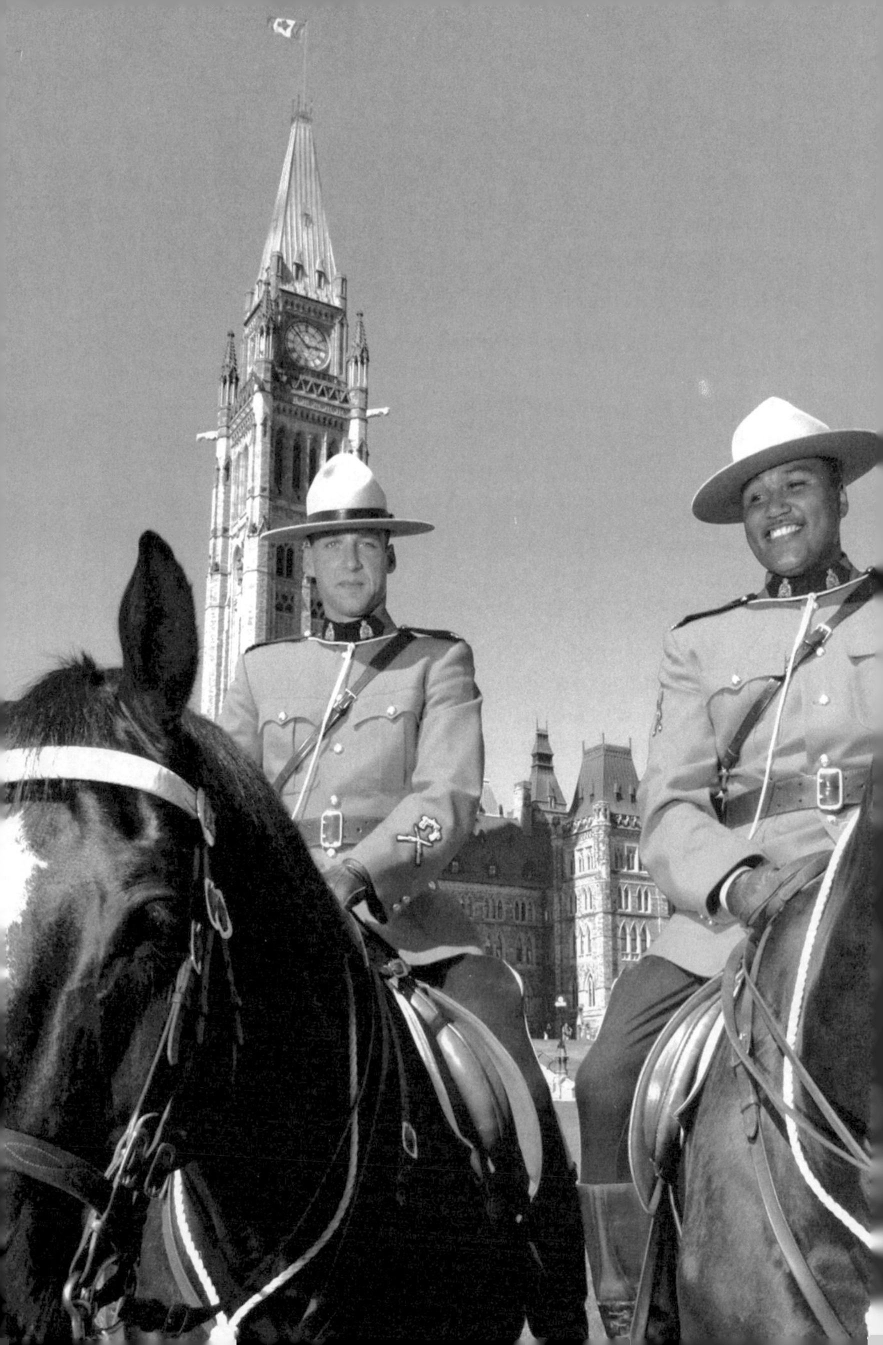

Crime and Punishment

CRIMELINE

1826: By default, Lt.-Col. John By becomes the first Justice of the Peace because he is the area's only legal authority. Royal Engineers become de facto policemen.

1835: The Bytown Association for the Preservation of the Public Peace is formed. Despite this, during the early 1840's, the "brawling, rioting and lusting community of Bytown" became known as the most feared community in North America.

1849: Stony Mountain Riots have Tories and Reformists battling each other. When the gunsmoke clears, one man is dead and more than two dozen are wounded.

1855: Roderick Ross is appointed the first Police Chief. He has 17 constables. Pay is piecework, based on the number of arrests.

1862: Nicholas Street Gaol is built.

1863: "Professional" police force is established.

1865: The first police station is constructed on the present site of the National Arts Centre.

1866: Members of the police force become salaried.

1868: Father of Confederation Thomas D'Arcy McGee is assassinated on an Ottawa street. Alleged Fenian James Whelan is later convicted of his murder.

1869: James Whelan is hanged at a public execution. Less than a year later, a ban on public executions is legislated. Whelan's ghost is rumoured to haunt the Nicholas Street Gaol building.

1913: Florence Campbell becomes Ottawa's first policewoman. In 1935, she retires and the position of policewoman is abolished.

1933: Convicted for murdering a gas station attendant during a robbery, William Seabrooke becomes the second man to be hanged at Nicholas Street Gaol.

1939: RCMP Equestrian Centre opens in Ottawa to stable and train horses for the Musical Ride.

1947: Member of Parliament Fred Rose is sentenced to six years for spying for the Soviet Union.

1966: Offices of the Cuban Trade Delegation are bombed.

1967: Yugoslav Embassy is bombed.

1970: A bomb planted in the National Defence Headquarters in downtown Ottawa kills Jeanne St. Germain. The case remains unsolved.

CRIME

1974: The Cuban Embassy is bombed.

1974: Patrick "Paddy" Mitchell, later to lead the Stopwatch Gang, masterminds a theft of 368 pounds of gold bullion from Ottawa International Airport, the largest gold heist in Canadian history.

1982: Turkish Commercial Counselor Kani Gungar is shot down at his home, paralyzed for life, while Turkish Military Attache Atilla Altikat is assassinated in his car while waiting at an Ottawa stoplight.

Take 5 FIVE OTTAWA COLD CASES

1. In December 1966, Rose Baillargeon was found strangled in the basement of her downtown apartment. Police are seeking an unknown male who may have left a fingerprint at the scene.

2. In January 1970, Wasil (William) Gubin was found dead in his Bank Street shoe store, apparently as a result of a robbery gone awry. The assailant(s) may have left blood at the scene due to cuts received breaking the glass in the store's front door.

3. In September 1990, the body of 16-year-old Melinda Sheppit was discovered in a ByWard Market parking lot. She had been strangled. Sheppit was last seen alive in the Market area earlier that day.

4. In December 1993, Sophie Filion was strangled and dumped in a Westboro parking lot. As with the Sheppit case, police have a possible suspect but lack sufficient evidence to press charges.

5. In September 1995, Carrie Mancuso was found asphyxiated in her Vanier apartment. She was last seen alive in the ByWard Market area accompanied by a man wearing a kilt. Like Sheppit and Filion, Mancuso was known to work as a prostitute.

1985: Extremists blow off the front door of the Turkish Embassy, seize hostages and kill a Canadian security guard.

1988: Ottawa-based American fugitive Gilbert Galvan, alias Robert Whiteman, is sentenced to twenty years in prison for a cross-country armed robbery spree that totaled more than $2.3 million.

1992: The Iranian Embassy is attacked by Iraqi religious extremists.

1994: Dr. Nicholas Battersby is gunned down in Ottawa's first daylight random drive-by shooting. Two young offenders are convicted.

1995: Popular TV sportscaster Brian Smith is fatally shot by a killer with a grudge against the media. Jeffrey Arenburg is subsequently committed to a mental institution.

1996: The Champagne Gang, four high-living young Ottawans, are arrested in St. Catharines. They later plead guilty in a plea bargain to 54 of an estimated 200 burglaries, netting $1.5 million. Each receives a sentence of two years less a day.

1999: Former OC Transpo employee Pierre Lebrun fatally shoots four OC Transpo workers, then commits suicide.

2000: The National DNA Data Bank officially opens on the site of the RCMP Headquarters complex.

2004: A house firebombing kills two children. Four people are subsequently convicted on a variety of charges, including capital murder and accessory after the fact.

2008: The Ottawa Police Service introduce a new Google-based crime mapping tool to allow residents to look up police calls for service in neighbourhoods across Ottawa.

CRIME

2014: RCMP lay 31 criminal charges involving expense scandal against Senator Mike Duffy.

2015: Duffy's trial begins. He pleads not guilty to all 31 charges.

2016: Senator Mike Duffy found not guilty on all 31 charges.

OTTAWA CASUALTIES IN THE LINE OF DUTY
- Constable Jeffrey Armstrong: January 11, 1940 - May 13, 1963
- Constable George Constantineau: August 14, 1915 - November 17, 1954
- Constable Harold Dent: March 2, 1903 - June 20, 1940
- Constable David Kirkwood: October 26, 1955 - July 11, 1977

Scandal in the Senate

Michael Dennis "Mike" Duffy is a Canadian senator and former Canadian television journalist. Prior to his appointment to the upper house in 2008, he was the Ottawa editor for CTV News Channel. After resigning from the Conservative caucus on May 16, 2013 during a controversy over the expense claims filed by him and other Senators, Duffy sat in the Senate as an independent, representing Prince Edward Island, until the Senate voted on November 5, 2013. On July 17, 2014, Duffy was charged by the Royal Canadian Mounted Police with 31 offences. These included fraud, breach of trust and bribery. He was charged with fraud and breach of trust in relation to $80,000 in expenses that he claimed as a senator. Eighteen of the charges were laid in relation to $50,000 in travel expenses which Duffy claimed as a senator. Eight more charges of fraud and breach of trust were laid in relation to the alleged misuse of $60,000 in public funds for consulting contracts. The bribery charge was in relation to the $90,000 he received from Nigel Wright, Stephen Harper's then chief of staff. The trial began on April 7, 2015. Duffy was acquitted of all charges on April 21, 2016 and immediately resumed his seat in the Senate.

Calm, Cool, and Collecting

On January 14, 2007, Ottawa native son Patrick Michael "Paddy" Mitchell, the most flamboyant member of the Stopwatch Gang, died in a U.S. federal prison hospital at Butner, North Carolina. More than 200 people attended Paddy's wake in Ottawa, and every one of them had a good word for him.

Years before the Stopwatch Gang was given its name by a U.S. crime reporter, its members, Paddy, Steven Reid and Lionel Wright teamed up to carry off Canada's largest gold bullion robbery to that date (1974), a $700,000 haul from the Ottawa airport. By December 1979, the trio had been arrested on unrelated charges, escaped federal penitentiaries, and began an armed robbery career which would make them legends.

Traveling across the U.S., the gang racked up as many as 140 bank robberies, netting them more than $15 million. Planning and efficiency were the gang's hallmarks. Paddy was the idea man, Reid handled ways and means and Wright was the detail man. Together, they never fired a shot, never hung about inside a bank longer than two minutes (usually less), and were renowned for their politeness.

The gang topped the FBI's Most Wanted list but it took an informer to do them in. Reid and Wright went down first, while Paddy continued robbing banks until he was arrested under an alias in Phoenix. Before his real identity was discovered, Paddy made bail and disappeared. He was on the loose for another year, the FBI finally collaring him in Florida. Sentenced to 17 years in the Arizona State Prison, Paddy needed two years before he could escape. In 1986, he was gone again. By 1990, he was living in the Philippines, married and tending a newborn son.

After running out of cash, Paddy returned to the U.S. in 1995 where he was arrested after a $160,000 bank robbery in Southaven, Mississippi. He was sentenced to 65 years in federal prison. Unlike Reid and Wright, who had managed transfers to Canadian prisons, Paddy's application for transfer was repeatedly denied by U.S. authorities.

Reid and Wright were eventually released on parole. Reid went on to a writing career, married, and began a family. Drug abuse, however, proved to be his downfall. In 1999 he was sentenced to 18 years for a bank robbery in Victoria, BC. Wright did better. He settled down, reportedly becoming an accountant.

CRIME

Serenity Shattered

On August 11, 2003 a police cadaver dog found the nude, raped body of 27-year-old Ardeth Wood, a tragic end to the largest search operation ever mounted by the Ottawa police. Wood, a doctoral student in philosophy at the University of Waterloo, had been taking a break from her studies to visit her family in Orleans, a suburb of Ottawa. Shortly after lunch on August 6, she went for a bike ride along the scenic bike trail Aviation Parkway.

During the course of the investigation over 5,000 suspects were logged. To that avalanche police had to add names of over 1,000 known sexual offenders gleaned from their own records. Public and media pressure was enormous. The cycling paths, winding for many km along the waterways and through the Greenbelt were the jewels of the city but suddenly they were now a labyrinthine death trap.

Within days, a composite sketch of a suspect based on descriptions of several witnesses was circulated citywide. Moreover, he matched the description of a man who, since June, had been accosting female cyclists, attempting to lure them from the bike paths.

Among the overwhelming number of tips was one provided by Crime Stoppers on the day Wood's body was found. While it was anonymous, the call had come from a professional — perhaps a social worker — and was made more credible by the fact the caller had consulted with a lawyer before picking up the phone.

The information identified Chris Myers as a possible suspect. A superficial scan of Myers' criminal record turned up convictions for minor street level drug trafficking and threatening, so he was dismissed. Thousands of names were checked and hundreds of interviews were conducted. By process of elimination the name of 25-year-old Chris Myers was slowly making its way to the top of the list.

Then in May 2005, Myers shot to the top. North Bay police arrested him for sexual assault and promptly notified their Ottawa counterparts. Subsequent interrogation by Ottawa Police detectives led to Myers being charged with four sexual assaults that had occurred in Ottawa between July 2003 and December 2004. A full 806 days since Wood had first vanished, he was charged with her murder.

Crime Stoppers awarded the original tipster $1,000, but the cash was never picked up. The case was finally closed when Myers pled guilty on January 8, 2008.

Take 5: OTTAWA'S FIVE PARLIAMENTARY-STYLE POWER CORRUPTIONS

1. John A. MacDonald, Canada's very first Prime Minister, lost a re-election bid in 1874 over allegations of influence peddling in the awarding of the contract to construct the railway to the Pacific from the Ontario border. The contract went to a consortium that had contributed $350,000 to MacDonald's Conservative Party. No charges were laid.

2. In 1925, rum-running was a boom industry for Canadians. Prime Minister Mackenzie King's Minister of Customs and Excise, Jacques Bureau, in charge of keeping Canadian booze out of the U.S., was found to be doing all he could to get it in, to the point of pulling enforcement agents off the Quebec and Ontario borders. When Bureau resigned, King appointed him to the Senate. King's minority government fell, but he was re-elected soon after.

3. Britain had the Profumo Scandal — playgirls and (maybe) Soviet spies. In John Diefenbaker's government, Ottawa had the Gerda Munsinger Affair (1961). She was an East German playgirl and (maybe) Soviet spy. Gerda got to Canada's Associate Defence Minister Pierre Sevigny and Minister of Trade and Commerce George Hees. Sevigny left politics. Hees trucked on.

4. On average, Brian Mulroney lost one Cabinet Minister a year to various allegations. For example, his Minister of Regional Economic Expansion, Sinclair Stevens folded his tent and left town amid allegations . . . something about a $2.6 million loan to a Stevens family company. As if losing Ministers wasn't enough, one of his MP's, Michel Gravel, had to plead guilty to 15 counts of fraud and influence peddling. He was sentenced to four months in the slammer and fined $50,000.

5. 2004 was the year Jean Chretien's government and Paul Martin's election hopes were skewered by the Sponsorship Scandal, involving $150 million paid out to ad agencies to do little or no work. The only proviso to the agencies was that substantial amounts be kicked back to the Liberal Party, which, dutifully, they did. Some of the players ended in up jail, but the politicians managed to come away with little worse than besmirched reputations.

CRIME

Take 5 — TOP FIVE MOST STOLEN CARS IN OTTAWA

1. **2013 Cadillac Escalate**
2. **2010 Acura ZDX**
3. **2009 BMW X6**
4. **2003 Chevrolet Avalanche**
5. **2014 Acura MDX**

Source: Ottawa Police Services

- Constable John Maki: August 22, 1935 - April 4, 1966
- Constable John Montgomery: February 20, 1908 - July 31, 1931
- Constable Russell O'Connor: April 18, 1942 - September 7, 1983
- Detective Thomas Stoneman: February 18, 1908 - October 29, 1945
- Constable Kenneth Swett: March 8, 1951 - July 17, 1981
- Sergeant David Tuckey: March 29, 1933 - January 21, 1970
- Constable David Utman: August 11, 1945 - October 14, 1983
- Constable Ireneusz "Eric"Czapnik: May 26, 1958 - December 29,2009

CRIME

Ottawa has the 21st highest crime rate of all Canadian Census Metropolitan Areas (CMAs) with more than 100,000 people and takes 7th place among the nine Canadian CMAs with populations over 500,000. Ottawa's crime rate fell to 11 percent in 2013 and in 2015 fell another 2 percent to 9 percent.

In Ottawa, you're less likely to have your home broken into than if you were in Vancouver, Saskatoon, Regina or even St. John's.

Did you know...

. . . that at one time in the early history of Queenswood Heights, so many RCMP families lived on one street that it was nicknamed Scarlet Lane?

Did you know...

...that in 1977 a police raid on a prostitution ring turned up a prostitute's client book containing the names of a senior Ottawa Police official, a provincial court judge, several members of the RCMP and OPS, and an abundance of prominent politicians, businessmen, dignitaries and journalists? After a lengthy investigation and much clamour in the local press, no charges were laid.

VIOLENT CRIME (RATE PER 100,000 CITIZENS)
- Homicide: 0.7
- Attempted Murder: 1.4
- Assault (incl. Sexual Assault): 425
- Other Sexual Offences: 3
- Robbery: 53.8
- Abduction: 9

OTTAWA DRIVES
Flip the coin in Ottawa. The city has either the worst drivers in Ontario or the most efficient policemen and bylaw officers. In 2015, there were 824 Criminal Code traffic offences.

TRAFFIC CRIME AND ACCIDENTS BY THE NUMBERS (2006)
- 14,784 collisions
- 29 fatal collisions
- 3,598 non-fatal injuries
- 921 charges for driving with a suspended license

Did you know...

...that in response to 68,749 Priority One calls, police were at the scene within 8.9 minutes on average, well below the departmental standard of 15 minutes?

CRIME

- 625 cases of impaired driving
- 63 cases of dangerous driving
- 79 cases of failure to remain or stop

In a Day's Work

January 1955 was cold in Ottawa. The two men who broke into the Brink's Express Company office on Sparks Street, however, weren't just trying to get warm. What they had failed to realize was they were treading on Constable Tom Flanagan's turf. He was a policeman who believed that in his patrol area the crime rate should be zero.

He crept up the fire escape and slipped into the building. After disarming them, he held them at gunpoint until help arrived. In 1958, Flanagan was on the front page again. He had leapt into the frigid Rideau River just above Rideau Falls and saved a youth from going over the falls to his death. The river was in full spring run-off at the time, still cluttered with ice chunks and debris, but Flanagan battled through and made shore against the surging current near the crest of the falls.

As Flanagan made his way up through the ranks of the Ottawa Police Service(OPS), he also developed a reputation for coolness in crisis. In May 1976, OPS newly formed SWAT Team got its first call out when an armed man barricaded himself in his house after shooting at police. Then-Superintendent Flanagan calmly negotiated the man's surrender.

In 1979, when two long-time criminals grabbed three hostages, including a policeman, Flanagan again negotiated the release of the hostages and surrender of the offenders. As a result, he received Canada's second highest award for bravery, the Star of Courage. On July 1, 1989, Flanagan was appointed Ottawa's Police Chief.

When he officially retired after 42 years on the force, City Council declared March 31, 1993 Thomas G. Flanagan Day. Council also declared that the OPS headquarters be named the Thomas G. Flanagan Building. Tributes didn't stop there. Flanagan was presented with the Canada 125 Medal for community work from the Governor General.

Did you know...

...that the National DNA Data Bank contained 277,590 convicted offender and crime scene DNA profiles and had achieved 3,270 crime scene to offender matches. Five hundred-six hundred samples are received each week.

Source: OPS.

POLICING OTTAWA
- Ottawa has 1,300 police officers
- Gross expenditures for 2015: $269.8 million

Firebomb Murder For Hire

On the night of January 30, 2004, Molotov cocktails fashioned from gasoline-filled wine bottles and hurled into the living room of an Ottawa rowhouse resulting in the deaths of 7-year-old Cole Rodgers and his 10-year-old sister, Chelsea.

Four men were subsequently charged with murder and a woman was charged with manslaughter. Testimony indicated that one of the men, Randy Parish, struck a deal to pay the others $7,000 each to kill the children's mother, Cindy Rodgers. The children died in the inferno while their mother sought help from a neighbour.

The Crown alleged that Parish contracted the murder because Rodgers was damaging his neighborhood reputation by telling other local residents he was a pedophile. Indeed, the first prosecution trial witness was a local boy who accused Parish of sexually molesting him.

Parish, along with Ghassan Salah, was convicted of capital murder with no possibility of parole for 25 years. A third accused, Tom McDowell, was found guilty of non-capital murder, while the fourth, Steve Cameron, pleaded guilty and received a 23-year sentence.

The murder convictions are currently being appealed, based in part on defense contentions that the firebombs were only meant to frighten Rodgers into silence and, second, that Parish had assured his co-defendants that the children were not at home.

CRIME

SALARY

The Ottawa Police Service pay scale is competitive with other Canadian police services. The following is a breakdown of the salary range for the rank of constable. A constable's pay class increases on their anniversary date during the first three years of service.

Annually 2016:

- Rookie: $47,729.26
- 1st Class Constable: $93,000

Source: OPS

CRIME STOPPERS

In 2016, Ottawa's Crime Stoppers had recovered $280,218 in illicit drugs. It has recovered $37 million in stolen property and illicit drugs in its 23-year history. The organization had also paid out $13,900 in awards for the anonymous tips that helped police solve those crimes during 2016. There were a total of 4,245 new tips received, resulting in 206 new charges and two weapons seized.

Did you know...

. . . that Ottawa's first cold case murder occurred on September 9, 1913, when a bookmaker's clerk, Abe Rubenstein, (alias Charles Robinson) was discovered stabbed to death?

Did you know...

. . . that in 1970, Ottawa Police Service fired a new cadet because he stole a car to get to his police training classes on time?

Take 5: TOP FIVE PROPERTY CRIMES

1. **Theft Under $5000**
2. **Break and Enter**
3. **Fraud**
4. **Theft, Motor Vehicle**
5. **Possession, Stolen Goods**

Source: Ottawa Police Services.

FINE, THEN

- Using a closed road: $85
- Careless driving: $400
- Drive without proper headlights—commercial motor vehicle: $200
- Fail to surrender license: $85
- Drive motor vehicle, no plates: $85
- Fail to yield to pedestrian; $150
- Fail to report damaged vehicle: $140
- Fail to stop at red light: $260
- Fail to stop for school bus: $400
- Fail to stop for emergency vehicle: $400
- Fail to stop for school bus: $400

Source: Ontario Court of Justice.

Did you know...

... that Ottawa's public transit authorities have hired 41 special constables to keep the peace on the city's buses?

CRIME

Take 5 OTTAWA POLICE SERGEANT RON COOPER'S TOP FIVE
FRAUD SCAMS PLAGUING THE CITY

1. **Identity theft**
2. **Credit card skimming**
3. **Cheque forgery**
4. **Money wiring schemes**
5. **Internet-based fraud**

OTTAWA BY-LAW SERVICES

The City of Ottawa's By-law and Regulatory Services Branch is a uniformed municipal law enforcement agency which provides regulatory services to the residents of Ottawa. By-law services provides regulatory services to protect the public health, safety and property rights of citizens. Enforcement activities may include: yard maintenance, property standards and zoning, noise control, animal care and control, parking and traffic enforcement and business licensing. Call volumes for enforcement have increased over the years. In 2005, there were 53,718 by-law complaints. This increased to 73,000 by 2013. They may be due to addition of the 3-1-1 number to call.

Did you know...

. . . that during their first few armed robberies a Stopwatch Gang member always wore a stopwatch dangling from his neck, but the watch was never used?

Did you know...

. . . that in 2015 the Ottawa Police Service responded to 340,775 calls?

Take 5 — TOP FIVE CITIZEN NEIGHBOURHOOD POLICING CONCERNS

1. Speeding Cars
2. Break & Enter/Burglary
3. Vandalism to Property
4. Theft from Vehicles
5. Bicycle Theft

Source: Ottawa Police Service.

THE SORRY COP

In 1976, scandal rocked Ottawa's police force in east end Vanier when Vanier's Police Chief Claude Dwyer was found guilty of stealing $878.30 from the police force.

After an Ontario Provincial Police investigation, evidence showed Dwyer stole the money from a police safety deposit box. He was sentenced to six months in jail and fined $1,000.

In 1977, more charges were leveled against Dwyer. He was convicted of bribery and corruption when he was proven to have accepted a bribe from a local club owner to stave off criminal investigations. The club was alleged to be the hangout for an assortment of villains.

Dwyer's convictions were soon eclipsed when a prostitute's call book was discovered to contain names of many prominent local movers and shakers. The Vanier Police Department has since been merged into the OPS.

Did you know...

. . . that the patrol area of the Ottawa Police Service is approximately the geographic size of Prince Edward Island?

CRIME

Take 5 FIVE AGENCIES PROTECTING PUBLIC PEACE IN OTTAWA

1. **Ottawa Police Service**
2. **Royal Canadian Mounted Police**
3. **Canadian Security Intelligence Service (CSIS)**
4. **Canada Border Services Agency**
5. **Joint Task Force-2 (JTF-2)**

DRUG OFFENCES

Drug-related offences reported by Ottawa Police in 2015 were 188 per 100,000 population. However, if Ottawa-Gatineau is considered a unit, Gatineau's 287 per 100,000 would push the cross-river figure higher.

In that year, there were:
- Cannibas: 759 arrests
- Ecstacy: 6 arrests
- Crystal Meth: 7 arrests
- Herion: 7 arrests
- Cocaine: 334 arrests
- Other contraband: 177 arrests

Sources: Ottawa Police Service; Statistics Canada.

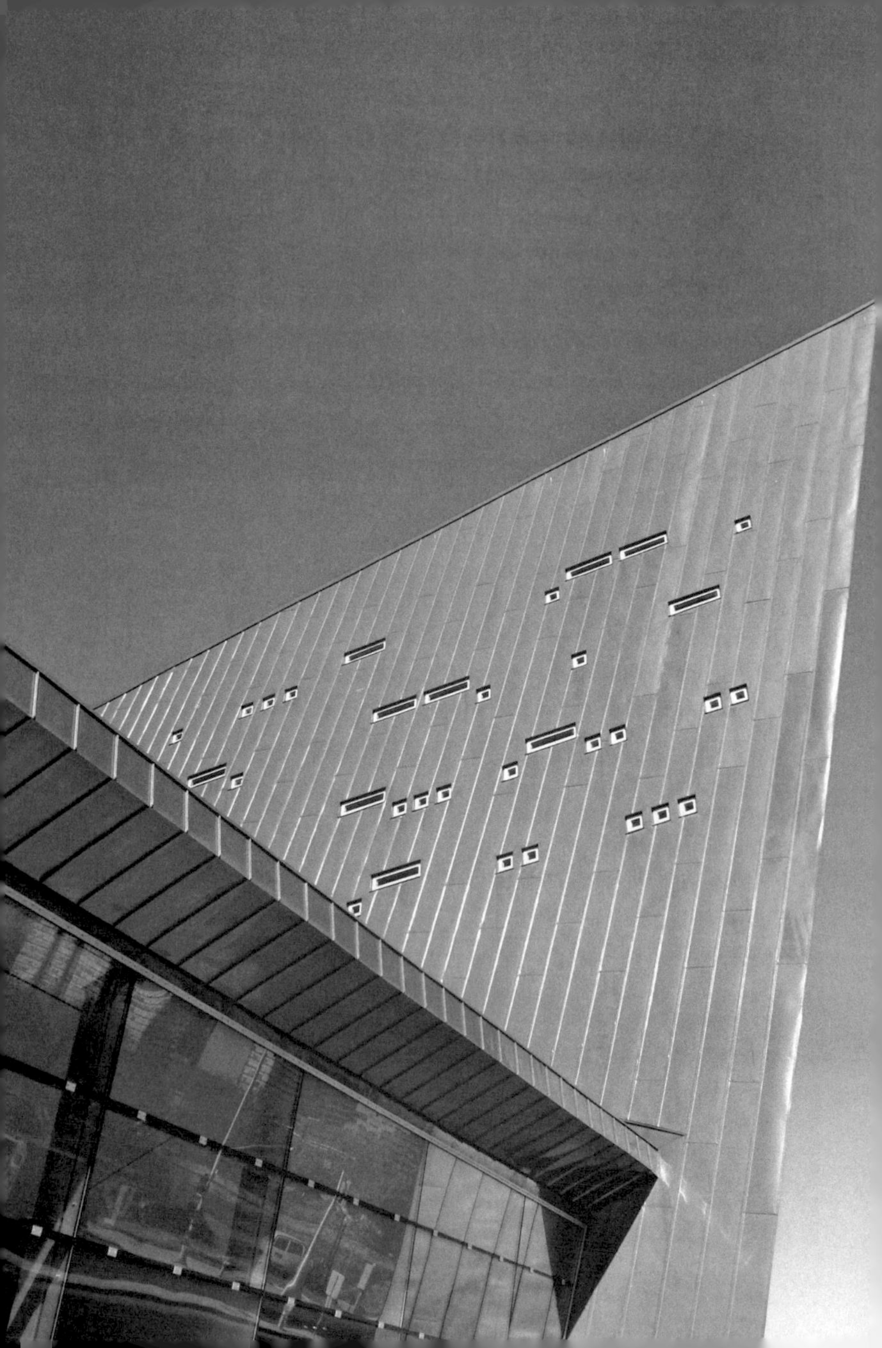

CULTURE

Culture

Like any city, Ottawa is a product of its contradictions. On the one hand, it is a white collar, civil service town; on the other hand, its most important historical influences are lumber and farming. Couple that with an upstart country with an upstart city determined to be a major player on the international stage, and you have the ingredients for an interesting cultural life. Cultural activity is acknowledged as a strong and efficient economic generator and the City now funds over 300 arts and heritage groups, festivals and artists annually. The Ottawa Cultural Alliance comprises umbrella organizations that have over 800 members across the city.

ARTISTS
- Number of artists in Canada: 136,600
- Number of artists in Ottawa: 6,000
- Average artists' salary in Ottawa: $32,800, the 2nd highest in Canada.
- 1 in 20 jobs in Ottawa are in culture

Source: Canada Council for the Arts.

CREATIVE NEIGHBOURHOODS
The highest concentration of artists in Ontario outside of Toronto is in Eastern Ottawa, which has 3.0% of its labour force in the arts — almost four times the national average. Other areas of Ottawa that are at least double the national average of 0.8% are:
- Ottawa West
- Wellington West
- Hintonburg
- the Glebe and South
- West Ottawa – Highland Park
- ByWard Market – Lower Town area
- Central Ottawa

Source: Hill Strategies Research Inc.

OTTAWA HAS
- 70 actors
- 360 artisans and craftspersons
- 60 conductors, composers and arrangers
- 275 dancers
- 855 musicians and singers
- 75 other performers
- 465 painters, sculptors and other visual artists
- 465 producers, directors, choreographers and related artists
- 1,775 writers

Source: Canada Council.

CULTURAL SPENDING
Ottawa residents' cultural spending ($1,064 per person) ranks first in Canada. Total cultural spending was $890 million in Ottawa, including $450 million (51 percent) on home entertainment, $180 million (20 percent) on reading materials, $100 million (11 percent) on art works and events, $84 million (9 percent) on photographic equipment and services, $43 million (5 percent) on art supplies and musical instruments and

CULTURE

$45 million (5 percent) on movie theatre admissions. Ottawa residents spend $49 million on live performing arts.

Ottawa's local, non-profit cultural industry directly generates and spends $51 million in Ottawa collectively, annually. One dollar of municipal cultural investment directly leverages between $7-$10 from private sources.

Source: Hill Strategies Research Inc.

RECOGNITION OF THE ARTS

In 2012, the City approved a six-year, 2013-18 Cultural Action Plan, to be valued at $4,955 million. As of the end of 2016, only 22% or $1.1 million of planned investment is in place. The City of Ottawa's per capita investment in its local cultural sector is 31% below other cities. Investment is $7.22, compared to other major cities' average of $10.50.

- Provincial and Federal government investment: 11.1 million
- Private sector revenue (sponsorship, donations): 10.6 million
- Municipal government: 7 million

Source: Canada Council for the Arts.

LIVE PERFORMANCES

Having the prestigious National Arts Centre (NAC) in your backyard virtually ensures a steady stream of outstanding live theatre. Throughout the year, the NAC offers an assortment of performances in English and French. Other notable local performance groups include the Great Canadian Theatre Company, La Nouvelle Scène, Le Groupe Dance Lab and Opera Lyra.

Did you know...

... that cellist Julian Armour was the brains behind the Ottawa International Chamber Music Festival in 1993? The festival began in 1994 to rave reviews, 12,000 listeners, and 22 concerts.

Take 5 FIVE PLACE TO SEE AND BE SEEN

American poet Emily Dickinson wrote, "The show is not the show, but they that go." To see and be seen on the rarified heights of Ottawa society, personal appearances at the following are recommended:
1. **The Rideau Club**
2. **Royal Ottawa Golf Club**
3. **Britannia Yacht Club**
4. **National Arts Centre** (main stage premiere performances)
5. **Opera Lyra** (premieres)

PUTTING ON THE RITZ

Ottawa's social upper crust isn't comprised of just people with old money and dot.com megabucks. Actually, it has four ingredients: old prominent families; senior high tech owners and executives; politicians and public service mandarins and foreign diplomats. These provide the stock from which Ottawa's doyennes draw their A-list for galas, balls, teas, charity events and receptions — the social whirl that defines who's who in the city.

Invited guests know they've "made it" when they walk into an event and see security staff wearing custom-made suits, instead of ill-fitting uniforms or black T-shirts with "SECURITY" stenciled across the back.

Did you know...

... that Governor General John Buchan, who established the annual Governor General Literary Awards, was the first GG to die in office? Buchan was also the author of the internationally famous spy thriller classic, *Thirty-nine Steps*.

CULTURE

Alanis Morissette

Born June 1, 1974, Alanis Morissette is Ottawa's most successful singing export since Paul Anka. Even before she became an international success, Morissette was a minor star in Ottawa. In the 1980s, the Glebe Collegiate student appeared on the popular local kid's show, "You Can't Do That On Television," released her first single, "Fate Stay with Me," and performed with Ottawa's famous Orpheus Music Theatre Society.

Although many people think *Jagged Little Pill* was Morissette's first record, in truth she made two previous albums under the name Alanis. Signed by MCA Records Canada in 1990, Morissette released the pop/dance-tinged record, Alanis, in 1991. The record was a smash hit in Canada and garnered the young singer three Juno award nominations in 1992. She followed up with the less successful *Now is the Time* in 1993. With her record contract complete, Morissette was already at a crossroads in her young career.

She left Ottawa in 1993 and roamed the continent in search of song-writing partners. In 1995, while in Los Angeles, she met one in Glen Ballard. The pair clicked immediately and put together the record, *Jagged Little Pill*. Neither musician had huge hopes for the record, but when the first single "You Oughta Know" started getting airplay in Los Angeles, the record took off. In the end, *Jagged Little Pill* sold more than 30 million copies worldwide, produced three number one singles ("You Oughta Know," "Hand in My Pocket" and "Ironic") and made the Ottawa girl an international superstar.

While Morissette has never reached the popularity and success of *Jagged Little Pill*, her six subsequent records have firmly established her on the world stage. Along the way, she has also stayed in touch with her Ottawa acting roots, appearing in numerous films and TV series (including "Curb Your Enthusiasm" and "Sex and the City").

ROMANCING THE ROYALS

Kings, queens, princes and princesses have been beating a path to Ottawa since 1860. Most, of course, have been British but they have also arrived from Russia, Japan, Romania, Greece, Austria, Netherlands, Norway, Sweden, Luxembourg, Austria, Yugoslavia, Belgium, Monaco, Denmark, Thailand and Siam.

Ottawans owe it all to Queen Victoria who, for reasons known only to her, designated Ottawa as the capital city of British domains in North America and installed a Governor General. Almost immediately, Rideau Hall, the home of the Governor General, became the center of Ottawa's social universe. Unlike today when many scheduled events at the Hall are open to the public, to be "received" at Rideau Hall by the Governor General or his wife was the foremost social honour to which Ottawans could aspire. When living, breathing royals were on hand, the prestige attached to an invite was astronomical.

In 1878, the wife of the Governor General was Queen Victoria's daughter, Louise. That was a coming of age for Ottawans. In 1940 another hallmark was achieved, when Queen Victoria's granddaughter Alice accompanied her husband Prince Alexander to Ottawa when he was appointed GG.

CANADIAN TULIP FESTIVAL

The roots of Ottawa's Tulip Festival go back to the Second World War when Princess Juliana of the Netherlands donated over 100,000 tulip bulbs to Canada as an appreciation for the help Canada provided the Dutch during the war.

When the Dutch monarchy fled to Canada and the third child Margriet was born, the Parliament of Canada passed a special law

Did you know...

. . . that at 103 years of age, Ottawa's Orpheus Musical Theatre Society is North America's oldest musical theatre group?

CULTURE

Take 5 LEE DEMARBRE'S FIVE BEST PLACES TO SHOOT IN OTTAWA

Lee Demarbre is an award-winning Ottawa filmmaker best known for his hilarious, campy horror/action/musical films like *Jesus Christ Vampire Hunter* (2001) and *Harry Knuckles and the Treasure of the Aztec Mummy* (1999).

1. **The Royal Alexandra Interprovincial Bridge** crosses the Ottawa River just east of Parliament Hill at Nepean Point in Ottawa. Buster Keaton shot The Railrodder there — that's good enough for me. The bridge is featured in the short film *Harry Knuckles and the Treasure of the Aztec Mummy*.

2. **G & L Auto Repairs and Recycling**. If a car is wrecked in Ottawa it ends up here piled on top of hundreds of other wrecked cars. This location looks like the final scene of every contemporary martial arts film you've ever seen. Warning: if you shoot here, get your tetanus shots.

3. **Morrison's Quarry** (Wakefield, Quebec) Just a 20-minute drive from downtown Ottawa, this location is great for dream sequences and anything surreal. The location has white sand and rock, towering cliffs, underwater wreckage and crystal clear ponds shaded light blue. You'll think you're on Mars. Featured in the short film series *Harry Knuckles and the Siege of the Leopard Lady* (2003).

4. **Meech Lake** (the north-east section of the lake, a 10 minute walk down the path of the O'Brien Beach parking lot, to be more specific.) There's a dam at this location separating the lake from a pond and beach area. It's a magnificent view and an endless inspiration for a filming location. Best of all; the area is the oldest nudist beach in all of Canada (60 years a nude beach!). On a good day of location scouting you could bump into some hikers wearing nothing but their birthday suits. Featured in the films *Harry Knuckles* (1998) and *Harry Knuckles and the Pearl Necklace* (2004).

5. **The Dominion Tavern** (33 York St. in the ByWard Market.) Simply the bar with the most character in Ottawa. No Hollywood studio could ever set dress a bar with as much personality. Featured in every one of my movies — there's still blood stains on the ceiling in the men's washroom from *Jesus Christ Vampire Hunter*.

declaring Princess Juliana's rooms at the Ottawa Civic Hospital to be Dutch territory so that the infant would have exclusively Dutch, and not dual nationality.

Held every spring, the Canadian Tulip Festival is the largest of its kind in the world. The festival showcases millions of tulips throughout Ottawa and also features an array of outdoor concerts. The largest collection of tulips is featured at the Commissioner's Park by Dow's Lake.

POLITICS AIN'T THE ONLY THING CARTOON IN TOWN

Ottawa has a thriving film community, especially in animation. Norman McLaren headed up the animation department of the National Film Board of Canada in 1942 and made many of his award winning films in Ottawa. Since then, Ottawa has been home to many famous studios

Take 5 FIVE GG CONTRIBUTIONS

We tend to think of our Governor Generals as figureheads hanging about to remind us of our ties to the former British Empire. The truth is their influence as social arbiters have been enormous, and many of them have contributed hugely to Canadian culture as we know it today. Among their contributions and those of their wives to Canada are:

1. **National Council of Women**, Victorian Order of Nurses and the Vanier Institute of the Family.
2. **Dominion Drama Festival**, Canada Council, National Art Gallery and National Library
3. **The annual Honours Roll**
4. **Royal Society of Canada**
5. Last, but not least, the **Stanley Cup** for hockey, the **Grey Cup** for football and the **Minto Cup** for lacrosse.

Incidentally, the Swedish tutor of one Governor General's children is believed to have introduced skiing to Canadians.

CULTURE

They Said It

> "If it hadn't been for Carleton [University], The Blues Brothers movie would never have been made."
>
> – Dan Aykroyd

(Crawley Films) and co-ops (IFCO, Saw Video Gallery). Ottawa also hosts the Ottawa International Animation Festival. Founded in 1976, the festival is the largest animation event in North America.

OH DANNY BOY

Dan Aykroyd's grandfather was an RCMP officer and his father was a policy advisor to Prime Minister Pierre Trudeau. Aykroyd attended three Ottawa schools, including Lisgar Collegiate, St. Pius X and St. Patrick's.

He was briefly tossed out of St. Patrick's for dressing up a pig like the Pope and bringing it to school for show and tell. He attended Carleton University to study criminology but subsequently dropped out.

Take 5 FIVE CULTURAL FESTIVALS IN OTTAWA

1. **TD Canada Trust Ottawa International Jazz festival,** a 10-day celebration of jazz music in the heart of Ottawa.
2. **Cisco Blues Festival**, although they use the term 'blues' loosely (in 2006, K.C. and the Sunshine Band played). The Blues Festival is a fantastic 10-day celebration of music.
3. **Ottawa International Chamber Music Festival**, the largest chamber music festival in the world and one of Canada's most important cultural events.
4. **Ottawa International Animation Festival** is the largest of its kind in North America.
5. **Ottawa Fringe Festival** is a unique, uncensored festival of variety, music, comedy and theatre featuring over 300 performers.

Take 5 — FIVE TV/FILM PERSONALITIES FROM OTTAWA

1. **Rich Little**, celebrity impersonator/impressionist; mimics over 200 voices.
2. **Lorne Greene**, actor; former CBC announcer hit the big time on TV shows, *Bonanza* and *Battlestar Galactica*.
3. **Dan Aykroyd**, actor/comedian; best known for his roles on *Saturday Night Live* and in the blockbuster hit, *The Blues Brothers*.
4. **Matthew Perry**, actor; most famous for his starring role on the hit TV show, *Friends*.
5. **Sandra Oh**, actress; well-known Canadian actress who hit stardom for her role in the film, *Sideways* and her starring role on popular TV series, *Grey's Anatomy*.

After doing acting and comedy in various Ottawa theatre groups, Aykroyd went on to join Toronto's Second City comedy troupe. From there he was recruited by fellow Canadian Lorne Michaels to join the cast of a new sketch comedy show called Saturday Night Live (SNL).

He stayed with SNL for four years, moving on to win an Emmy award for his outstanding writing and then starring in blockbuster after blockbuster.

MOVIE BUSINESS
- Number of movie theatres in Ottawa: 19
- Number of drive-ins: 1

Did you know...

... that Bryan Adams, Daniel Lanois, Bredan Fraser, Matthew Perry, Tom Green, Tom Cruise, and Alex Trebek all attended schools in Ottawa?

CULTURE

A Beaver Tale

Some things become part of the cultural fabric of a place, and nobody is exactly sure why or how. All they know is they like it. Elephant ears, whale tails, frying saucers and zeppole are some of the names given to deep fried, somewhat flattened pieces of bread dough. They fill, probably fatten, probably play hell with cholesterol counts, and, if Grant Hooker has his way, they'll become known throughout the world as BeaverTails.

When the dough hits the hot fat, it puffs up slightly and spreads into a flattish shape that, with a little imagination, resembles a beaver's tail. Slather that with cinnamon or powdered sugar, fruit compote, maple butter, caramel sauce, whipped cream and chocolate, and indulge — this is Ottawa's hearty helping of decadent fast food.

Grant Hooker started selling his BeaverTails from a small booth in Ottawa's ByWard Market in 1978. Then he set up on the ice of the Rideau Canal. BeaverTails became the ultimate comfort food for frigid skaters. The variety of available toppings may have increased, but the BeaverTails have remained as consistent as Big Macs. Still, BeaverTails have never been specially super-sized — they started out that way.

Over 30 years have passed. As the business grew, BeaverTails Canada Inc. was formed. It's still a family business, though now it's an Ottawa institution right up there with the Parliament Buildings. While they still maintain the ByWard Market shop, the Hookers have licensed BeaverTails to more than 130 outlets in Canada as well as seven other countries.

The ObamaTail is the newest selection, made in honour of the US President's first visit to Ottawa in 2009. The ObamaTail is made with cinnamon, sugar, whipped cream, then drizzled with chocolate, and sports a large frosting 'O'. As it turned out, President Obama made a stop at the ByWard Market on his way to the airport for this special treat.

Museum Central

The capital region is home to 29 major museums, including 12 national museums and institutions. Many of these attractions line Confederation Boulevard, "Canada's Discovery Route," which links Quebec and Ontario and is the site of a variety of events which animate the capital throughout the year. The architecture of Ottawa's museums, the copper roofs and the Gothic towers of Canada's national symbols are intriguing to gaze upon.

CANADIAN WAR MUSEUM
One of Ottawa's oldest museums (dating back to 1880) just underwent a major facelift. After nearly 40 years in a dingy old archives building on Sussex, the brand spanking new war museum opened in May 2005 at Lebreton Flats. The new space is significantly bigger, and features a dramatic architectural design by Raymond Moriyama based on the theme of regeneration. Moriyama's building incorporates themes of war with environmentally sound features like the use of recycled materials and a green roof composed of 10,684 square metres of various tall-grass species.

NATIONAL GALLERY OF CANADA
Even if you're not a fan of art stuff, you gotta at least check out the National Gallery of Canada building. Situated across from Major's Hill Park and designed by renowned architect Moshe Safdie, the Gallery building is a work of art in itself, composed of glass (bomb proof, of course, because it sits next door to the U.S. Embassy) and granite and highlighted by a glass tower that overlooks the city. Featuring a solid collection of Canadian art and hosting regular traveling exhibitions, the inside of the Gallery isn't too shabby either.

MUSEUM OF CIVILIZATION
Just across the bridge from the National Gallery in Gatineau, Quebec is the ever-popular Museum of Civilization. In fact, it's actually three museums. The Canadian Postal Museum, and the superb Canadian Children's Museum (which lets kids imagine they are visiting different

times in history) are also housed in this distinct building designed by Douglas Cardinal. The museum's curved design attempts to capture the uniqueness and randomness of the Canadian landscape.

MUSEUM OF NATURE
An often-overlooked member of Ottawa's museum family is the Museum of Nature, located in the Victoria Memorial Museum Building, otherwise known as "the castle." Built to mirror Canada's Parliament Buildings, this sandstone construction was completed in 1905. Inside visitors will find four floors of natural — and perhaps supernatural - history. It's long been rumoured that ghosts occupy the building's top floor.

CANADIAN AVIATION MUSEUM
Part of the Canadian Museum of Science and Technology (which is an anomaly in town as its building isn't much to look at), the Canadian Aviation Museum is located at Rockcliffe Airport. Housed in re-designed airplane hangars, the museum hosts one of Canada's finest collections of airplanes. During the summer you can even take a flight on some vintage airplanes.

CANADIAN AGRICULTURAL MUSEUM
Locally known as the Experimental Farm — and no, they don't do evil experiments on animals — the Agricultural Museum is a working farm right in the heart of Ottawa. At the museum, you can see a selection of barnyard creatures from cows and horses to rabbits, pigs, chickens and goats.

CUMBERLAND HERITAGE VILLAGE MUSEUM
You won't find this listed in most Ottawa tourist books, but the Heritage Museum, located 20 km east of Ottawa in Cumberland Village, is one of the most interesting and best kept secrets. This outdoor summer museum features 28 historical buildings including an operating sawmill, schoolhouse, farmsteads, a fire hall, train station, and church. A great place to get a vivid taste of Ottawa's rural past.

CORNISH

Ottawa-born Gene Cornish was the lead guitarist of successful American pop band The Young Rascals. Between 1966 and 1971, he recorded eight albums and more than a dozen singles with the group, including "Groovin'," "A Beautiful Morning" and "People Got To Be Free." In 1997, as part of the Rascals, he was inducted into the Rock & Roll Hall of Fame.

BEING GREEN

The roots of Tom Green's comedy began when he was a student at Algonquin College. He originally began hosting a rap show on the University of Ottawa's CHUO-FM, but soon turned it into a call-in show called The Midnight Caller Show. The premise, if there was one, was that listeners would call in and be insulted by Green and his colleague Glenn Humplik. The show had a cult following in Ottawa and paved the way for Green's first attempt at TV.

The Tom Green Show first appeared in 1995 on a local Rogers cable station. Fusing Green's love of Monty Python and David Letterman, the Tom Green Show was a strange brand of absurdist comedy. Within a year, the Tom Green Show was picked up by Canada's Comedy Network, quickly becoming their top rated program. U.S. fame quickly followed when Green was picked up by MTV.

GET STUFFED

Dining in Ottawa is a lot like politicians; there are plenty of good ones and some stinkers. To get a taste of political food, check out the Parliament Pub on Sparks Street and try Paul Martin's Everything for Everyone Sun-Dried Tomato Pizza or Stephen Harper's Right-Wing Voodoo Chicken Sandwich.

Did you know...

. . . that Paul Anka's hit song "Diana" was an ode to his Ottawan baby-sitter?

CULTURE

They Said It

> "I got booked into this place in Quebec, and when I started my act, I discovered that no one in the audience understood English. It was strictly a French-speaking audience. I did walks . . . Jack Benny's walk, Bob Hope's walk, John Wayne's walk. They all walk the same in French as in English."
>
> – Rich Little

For the apolitical, check out The Manx on Elgin Street for great pub food. If you like formal without the formality of a formal, stroll by the excellent Black Tomato in the ByWard Market. Locally owned, the Black Tomato has a fine menu, great beer and they even sell cds.

If Asian is your thing, stroll over to Bronson and Somerset where you'll find some fantastic Vietnamese restaurants. If dining's not your thing, you can get drunk good and fast at the lively Dominion Tavern, which has replaced the infamous "Laff" as the best bar/dive.

RIDEAU 175

This achievement has already provided a modest, typically Canadian boost to Ottawa's economy. A local craft brewery, Heritage Brewery, is marketing a limited edition commemorative beer named Rideau 175, available only in outlets along the canal.

IT WORKS

Move over, McDonalds – a new burger joint has moved into town. THE WORKS is a gourmet burger shop with an award-winning recipe – five locations, eight burgers, 66 toppings, and 528 combos. They claim to have the world's best burgers – and Ottawans everywhere agree.

Did you know. . .

> . . . that *Mr. and Mrs. Bridge* starring Paul Newman and Joanne Woodward was partially shot in Ottawa?

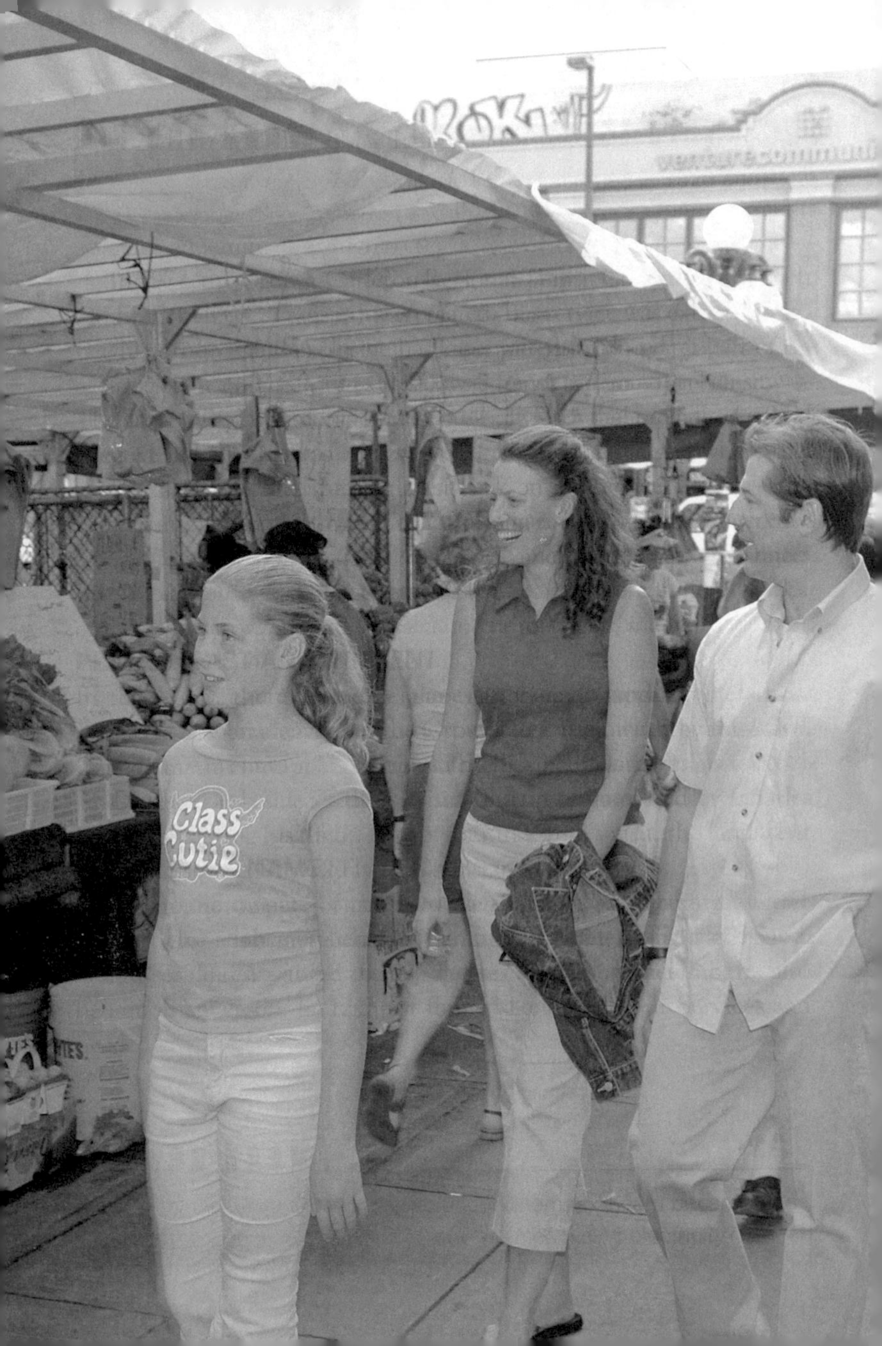
Class
Cutie

Economy

Ottawa's regional Gross Domestic Product is at $58.2 billion annually. Rumblings several years ago that the importance of the federal government to the economy here would be supplanted by the new to high tech sector were, of course, overblown. Ottawa is still a G-town, and it is government employment and expenditures that continue to offer stability and drive the economy.

Although high technology as a sector now has a larger share of the GDP (federal crown and some government research institutions also included), the federal government accounts for more than 120,000 jobs versus the high tech sector total of 75,000. Ottawa saw an increase of 9,000 federal government jobs in 2016, while Gatineau had an increase of 5,000. This was not related to the census. Together the one-two punch of the government and high technology account for 40 percent of Ottawa's total (GDP).

Did you know...

... that the Ottawa Chamber of Commerce (formerly the Ottawa Board of Trade) has been committed to the well-being of the city since 1857? In 1910, they even helped save the Rideau Canal from demolition.

GROSS DOMESTIC PRODUCT
Industry sector as a percentage of total GDP
- High tech: 18.9*
- Federal government: 18.2
- Tourism: 2.1
- Health and education: 7.5
- Finance, insurance, real estate: 10.4
- Trade: 9.4
- Construction: 4.0
- Primary (mainly rural output): 0.9
- Others: 28.6

*Note that high technology does include some government related crown organizations and corporations.
Source: City of Ottawa.

ONTARIO TAXES
- Provincial sales tax: 8 percent
- Federal GST: 5 percent
- Personal income tax rates: 9.15-12.16% percent of taxable income
- Small business corporate tax rate: 4.57-11.5% percent

Sources: Province of Ontario Ministry of Revenue; Canada Customs and Revenue Agency.

TAX FREEDOM DAY
The Fraser Institute's annual prediction of Tax Freedom Day is almost as much an event to Ontarians as the emergence of Wiarton Willie on Groundhog Day. In 2016, Tax Freedom Day fell on June 7th. On that day the tax collectors deemed their vaults full, for the time being anyway. Here's how the rest of the country stacked up:

- Nationally   June 17
- Alberta   May 17
- Saskatchewan   June 1
- Prince Edward Island   June 1
- **Ontario**   **June 5**
- British Columbia   June 5

ECONOMY

- Manitoba — June 7
- Nova Scotia — June 9
- New Brunswick — June 11
- Quebec — June 13
- Newfoundland and Labrador — June 14

Average personal income per capita: $46,049

Personal disposable income (after taxes): $35,000

Median family income (married couple families): $102,020

COST OF LIVING

Ottawa's cost of living is among the lowest at all salary levels, according to a North American survey that compared the total cost of living. It is 10% lower than in Toronto and has the third lowest mortgage rate in percentages. See table below which shows the family income required in each city to maintain the standard of living associated with three income scenarios (60K, 80K and 100K).

Sources: MMK Consulting and Runzheimer Canada.

INCOME LEVEL

CITY	$60,000	$80,000	$100,000
Edmonton	$61,830	$81,142	$99,902
Calgary	$62,818	$82,109	$105,317
Ottawa	$63,168	$84,102	$104,699
Montreal	$68,167	$92,594	$113,884
Vancouver	$69,009	$90,927	$112,647
Toronto	$74,114	$96,439	$122,627
Seattle	$73,723	$98,441	$118,048
Boston	$84,896	$112,115	$133,384
San Jose	$101,077	$144,029	$164,435

Sources: MMK Consulting and Runzheimer Canada.

Take 5 FIVE OTTAWA HOURLY SALARIES

1. Erik Karlsson, Ottawa Senators: $3,250
2. Ottawa City Manager: $166
3. Ottawa Chief of Police: $102
4. Ordinary Members of Parliament: $84.89
5. Ottawa Mayor: $75

Based on a 37.5 hour work week.

TOP TEN HOUSEHOLD EXPENDITURES

1. Personal income taxes: $15,526
2. Shelter: $19,197
3. Transportation: $11,812
4. Food: $8,475
5. Insurance premiums and pension contributions: $4,754
6. Recreation: $3,788
7. Household operation: $4,788
8. Clothing: $3,685
9. Gifts of money and contributions: $2,344
10. Household furnishings and equipment: $2,137

Source: Statistics Canada; City of Ottawa.

HOUSING MARKET

According to the Canadian Mortgage and Housing Corporation:
- The 2016 rental vacancy rate stood at 3 percent, down from 3.4 percent the year before.
- Average rent for a two bedroom apartment: $1,315 monthly
- Average house price increase in December 2016: 8%
- Number of residential properties sold in 2016: 15,537
- Average price of a resale house in November 2016: $401,626
- Average price of a condominium in 2016: $260,982

ECONOMY

You Said How Much?

Below are average wages for select jobs in Ottawa, drawn from the latest available data from Service Canada.

Engineering Manager:	$62.00
University Professors:	$40.00
Personal support Worker:	$16.65
Dental Hygienists:	$32.45
Administrative Assistants:	$16.33
School Teachers:	$31.00
Licensed Practical Nurses:	$24.33
General Office Clerks:	$18.35
Early Childhood Educators:	$17.00
Bus Drivers / Transit Operators:	$15.00
Security Guards:	$11.85
Hairstylists and Barbers:	$11.35

COST OF A HOUSE
Ottawa
Standard Condo: $260,982
Detached Bungalow: $364,851
Standard 2 Storey: $417,920
Standard Townhouse: $420,000

Source: Royal LePage.

Did you know...

... that trendy upscale Westboro was known to the residents of 1950s Hintonburg (now an artsy upstart neighbourhood) as "Mortgage Heights"? Hintonburgers had proudly built their houses little by little, as they could afford to add rooms, and viewed the practice of borrowing to build with deep suspicion.

HOUSING

Low income families and the homeless, bottoming out Ottawa's economic prosperity, remain a dilemma for city fathers. In 2016, (15 percent) were identified by Statistics Canada as low income in Ottawa. The average monthly income assistance is $656 monthly. Six hundred Ottawans were living on the street, 6,705 were living in shelters, and 6,825 accessed emergency shelters.

Sources: City of Ottawa; Statistics Canada.

RENTING

Average Rent ($ Dollars)

City	2 bedrooms	3 bedrooms
Halifax	$1,080	$1,295
Montreal	$1,200	$1,500
Calgary	$1,245	$1,499
Ottawa	**$1,320**	**$1,553**
Toronto	$1,650	$2,000
Vancouver	$2,000	$2,789

Source: Canada Mortgage and Housing Corporation.

IN OTTAWA . . .

- More than one third of renters in Ottawa pay more than 30 percent of their income for rent, which means that they have less money for food, clothing, education and other essentials.
- The Ottawa Community Housing Corporation is responsible for about 15,000 affordable housing units and is the second-biggest landlord in Ontario.
- In Ottawa, there are more than 32,000 seniors, parents, children, couples, singles and people with special needs who live in Ottawa City housing.

ECONOMY

Gates Crasher

Michael Cowpland was born and raised in England, and moved to Ottawa at the age of 21 to obtain his PhD at Carleton. At the height of the technology boom in the 1990s, he and his wife, Marlen, sat atop of the Ottawa social strata. Marlen Cowpland hosted a TV talk show that highlighted her taste in haute couture and showcased her purple-dyed Maltese dog, Bunny, while her husband portrayed the image risk taking, high-energy entrepreneur.

Michael Cowpland made a statement, daring to go head to head with Bill Gates. While he didn't succeed, there was a time when he gave Gates a serious run for his money.

Before he entered the software marketplace in 1985, Cowpland had already made his mark in the high-tech hardware development sector. With a PhD in electrical engineering, he was snapped up by telecom giant, Bell Northern Research. He then moved on to Micro Systems International.

At Micro Systems, Cowpland met an ambitious Welsh lad named Terence Matthews. Together they founded Mitel. Cowpland was Mitel's CEO for a decade. By 1985, the company had achieved world leadership in the design and manufacture of telecom-integrated circuit devices and electronic private switchboards. That year, control of Mitel was purchased by British Telecom.

Almost immediately, Cowpland started the Corel Corporation, competing directly with Microsoft. Within 15 years, Corel's two main products — CorelDraw and WordPerfect - had 50 million users worldwide. In the end, however, the competition was too much. Cowpland was investigated by the Ontario Securities Commission amid allegations he had used insider information to sell Corel shares before the company posted disappointing results. Cowpland stepped down as CEO in 2000.

Within a year, still based in Ottawa, Cowpland purchased controlling interest in Zim Corporation, a company built on two-way text messaging for business use. As for Corel, it was wholly acquired by Vector Capital, a private equity firm, for a price of $1 a share.

LABOUR DATA
Total Experienced Labour Force: 768,400

WORK FORCE COMPOSITION SAMPLE
By Industry
- Construction: 24,429
- Health and social assistance: 55,865
- Education: 36,308
- Finance and real estate: 25,000
- Federal government: 121,885
- Other: 29,871

By Occupation
- Accommodations: 36,019
- Business, finance and administration occupations: 122,400
- Natural and applied sciences and related occupations: 75,815
- Management occupations: 75,810
- Information and Culture: 15,226
- Trades, transport and equipment operators and related occupations: 52,005
- Professional, Scientific and Technical: 55,745
- Health occupations: 28,175
- Art, culture, recreation and sport: 11,127
- Occupations unique to primary industry: 6,575

Source: Statistics Canada.

ECONOMY

Just the Right Tool

Lee Valley Tools Ltd. was started in 1978 on Leonard Lee's Ottawa kitchen table. Lee had been carving out a successful future as a career civil servant with the federal Department of Industrial Development. If career and life are a marriage, Lee had decided a divorce was in order. He was seeking a new bride. He found one in the name of Lee Valley Tools.

Contrary to one urban legend in Canada, federal civil servants can have vision and passion. Lee's passion was woodworking and his vision included the probability that many other people shared this passion.

In 1978, Canadian consumers were not particularly confident in direct mail buying. Still, it was the most economical way for Lee to reach his market, buyers of specialized, high quality woodworking hand tools. Perhaps to hedge his projected bottom line, Lee included garden tools in his first catalogue. He also went with a proven seller, cast iron stove kits.

Now, nearly 30 years later, Lee Valley Tools mails three catalogues a year. Each catalogue offers more than 22,000 items, including some designed by the company engineers who have been operating as a spin-off business named Veritas Tools Inc.

In 2005, Veritas held 60 tool patents, most of which have been brought into production. Algrove Publishing Ltd. is another Leonard Lee company. Algrove has been publishing woodworking and gardening books since 1991.

Lee Valley Tools now grosses $50 million annually, has 500 employees and 13 retail outlets in Canada. Day to day operations have been turned over to his son, Robin, while the senior Lee moved on to other business opportunities. As he told the Globe & Mail writer Paul Lima, "I have a fear of mall walking."

THE OTTAWA COMMUTE
The average Canadian spends nearly 12 full days each year traveling between home and work, which works out to approximately 63 minutes a day.
- The average Ottawan commuted 7.8 km to work
- 69.6 percent of them did it in a car, truck, or van
- 20 percent used public transit
- 9.4 percent walked or cycled

Sources: City of Ottawa. Statistics Canada.

NO PARKING
- Median cost in Toronto: $325
- Median cost in Montreal: $296
- Median cost of monthly parking (unreserved rate) in Ottawa: $215
- Median cost in Vancouver: $296
- Median cost in Edmonton: $288
- Median cost in Calgary: $473

Source: Colliers International.

JOB GROWTH RATE
Ottawa-Gatineau added 44,358 new jobs from September 2008 to September 2015, an employment growth rate of 8.7. There were 9,600 created in the Capital Region in the 12 months to August 2016. The unemployment rate in 2016 was at 6.3%.

Did you know...

... that rain or shine, balmy or blizzardy, more Ottawans walk to work than do so in Vancouver, Montreal, Calgary, Edmonton or Toronto? Then, too, in winter, many Ottawans skate to work along the Rideau Canal.

ECONOMY

JOBS AND MORE JOBS
- The federal government and the high-technology sector may be the main employers in the city, but there are also more than 25,000 other employers in the city providing more than 500,000 jobs. There are 1,800 technology companies in Ottawa alone.

The Tiger That Roared

In May 1961, the Giant Tiger store was started in Ottawa. Giant Tiger's marketing principle was simple: "good quality at a fair price." The mark-up on products was always just a tad lower than the competition. Giant Tiger didn't take long to catch on with consumers.

As other low-end department stores such as Stedman's and Woolworth's declined, Giant Tiger grew, becoming a formidable beast in the department store jungle.

Turns out Gordon Reid did know a little something about retailing. When he started he had just $15,000 and a lot of nerve. The notion that it's better to earn 10 cents on an item ten times than $1 once seems to have worked. No one comes to Giant Tiger just once.

By 1968, Giant Tiger was successful enough to begin franchising stores. In 1977, stores were opened in Quebec. In 2001, a Master Franchise Agreement was signed with the North West Company, granting rights to open 72 Giant Tiger stores in western Canada. North West is no Johnny-come-lately on the department store scene. Overall, the company operates 206 stores in Canada and Alaska, with 8,000 employees, as well as a successful catalogue mail order business zeroing in on small remote communities. It grosses over 800,000,000 annually.

FEDERAL EMPLOYMENT

In Ottawa-Gatineau during 2016, federal government employment provided a living to 122,368 people. To put that in perspective, the next closest city was Montreal with 25,756. Additionally, Ottawa-Gatineau provided jobs for 16,000 provincial and municipal government employees.

Source: Statistics Canada.

COMMERCIAL REAL ESTATE

Vacancy rates continued to rise in south Ottawa to 6.5%, an area containing a mix of public- and private-sector tenants, unlike other areas were office space is dominated by the federal government or the tech sector.

DOWNTOWN OFFICE SPACE (COST PER SQUARE FEET)

- Calgary $45.68
- Montreal $48.28
- **Ottawa $49.34**
- Vancouver $52.72
- Toronto $68.19

- Class A downtown office space: $49 per square foot and rising.
- In the burbs the average is $25 per square foot but is expected by realtors to jump nearly 5 percent.

Sources: City of Ottawa. Statistics Canada.

SELF-EMPLOYMENT

Ottawa is in the lower end when it comes to self-employment. In all, 70.1 per 1,000 Ottawans work for themselves. Self-employment is a growing trend in Canada. Between 2008-2015, the number of self-employed Ottawans rose slightly by 2 percent.

ECONOMY

YOUTH ON OUR SIDE

Ottawa's entrepreneurial cohort has a strong future in large measure because of its youth. Compared to other major cities, it has a comparatively high proportion of self-employed people who are ages 15-35: 19.2 percent. Here's how other major cities stack up:

- Calgary: 20.1 percent
- Edmonton: 19.3 percent
- Montreal: 18.4 percent
- Toronto: 17.6 percent
- Vancouver: 16.3 percent

Silicon Valley North

Outside of the high technology industry in Canada, few people may have heard of Denzil Doyle. Inside it, he is a guru, the go-to guy for advice on how to start technology-based companies, sell their products and sustain their growth. He has been doing that successfully in Ottawa for fifty years. Shortly after graduating from Queens University with an engineering degree in 1956, Doyle joined a rising company named Computing Devices. He went on to start Digital Equipment Corporation, which at its height was grossing $160 million a year.

Since then, Doyle has been involved as an investor, director and leader of dozens of some Canada's biggest high tech success stories such as Newbridge Networks, a pillar of Ottawa's technology community. As chairman of Capital Alliance Ventures, he has overseen the investment of more than $40 million in over 30 companies in the telecommunications, software and semiconductor sectors.

Doyle continues to regard Ottawa as the place to be for tech-oriented entrepreneurs in Canada.

Take 5 OTTAWA'S TOP FIVE EMPLOYMENT SECTORS

1. **Federal, provincial and municipal governments jobs : 122,368**
2. **Retail: 58,582**
3. **Health: 55,865**
4. **Professional, scientific and technical workers :55,745**
5. **Education accounted for 35,308**

Source: City of Ottawa.

EMPLOYMENT GROWTH

In 2015, Ottawa-Gatineau had an employment growth level at 1.3%, and an employment growth rate of 1.1 in 2016. The unemployment rate in 2015 was 6.9 and 6.3 in 2016.

Source: Building Team Forecast

LABOUR MARKET

Ottawa's labour market added 2,500 jobs in July 2016, posting the sixth month consecutive monthly job increase. Local employment grew by 16,300 jobs from July 2015 to July 2016 and drove the unemployment rate down to 6.3 by mid- 2016.

Did you know...

. . . that although Canadian satirist and political pundit Allan Fotheringham called Ottawa "the town that fun forgot", in 2015 Ottawa attracted 5.5 million tourists?

Did you know...

. . . that median annual income for Ottawa workers is more than $5,000 higher than that for the rest of Ontario?

ECONOMY

They Said It

> "What was driving me crazy were the number of people who would say, 'I have 17 years, 8 months, 2 weeks, 2 days and 7 hours before I retire.' I'm sure shorter sentences were being served in Alcatraz at that time."
>
> **– Leonard Lee founder of Lee Valley and former civil servant**

INFRASTRUCTURE
AIR

Ottawa International Airport is Canada's 5th busiest air passenger terminal. The region is also served by the Carp Airport, which provides easy access to Ottawa's west end and the high concentration of high tech businesses, and the Gatineau Airport, serving cross-river western Quebec. All three airports can accommodate charter and corporate air traffic, and Ottawa also provides US Customs and Immigration pre-clearance facilities. When heads of state or kindred dignitaries fly to the capital, they often land at the military's Uplands Airport adjacent to the international facility.

Public transit and taxi services are available at the Ottawa International Airport, VIA Rail Station and Voyageur Bus Terminal. The taxi fare from the airport to downtown locations ranges from $25 to $30, plus gratuity.

Did you know...

. . . that only when the 1998 Ice Storm struck eastern Ontario and western Quebec did Ottawa EMO authorities calculate that, if ever isolated, Ottawa-Gatineau would have only a three day supply of food? In effect, much of what Ottawans would consume later that week would be either in warehouses in Montreal or Toronto or somewhere on the highways.

Take 5 — FIVE BUSINESSES TO WATCH
(OTTAWA'S TOP FIVE PRIVATELY HELD FASTEST GROWING COMPANIES OVER THE PAST THREE YEARS):

1. **You.I TV,** with a growth rate of 4,453%
2. **BBG Management Corp.,** at 2,033%
3. **NAPKYN,** at 985%
4. **Ontario Rental and Supply,** at 712%
5. **A Hundred Answers,** at 682%

Source: profitguide.com

RAIL

Ottawa Station was built in 1966, designed by John B. Parkin & Associates. The station is served for passengers by Via Rail inter-city trains that connect to both Montreal and Toronto. Canadian Pacific and Canadian National railways handle cargo and freight. The city has access to basically the entire continent by way of connecting lines.

The largest infrastructure project to date in Ottawa, the Confederation Line, at $2.1 billion is underway. As well, the Province of Ontario has invested in stage 2 of the Light Rail transit project.

HIGHWAY

Geographically, Ottawa is off the beaten track of the Trans Canada Highway but the region has direct four-lane highways that connect

Did you know...

... that the Union Bridge, a key part of the overall Rideau Project, a 202-foot wooden two-lane bridge at the Chaudiere Falls, designed by Lt.-Col. John By, and linking ByTown to Wrightsville, was the first constructed link between Upper and Lower Canada? Eventually it rotted away but it remains symbolic in Canada's history.

ECONOMY

They Said It

> "We are the capital of a G-8 nation — we deserve to walk with a swagger."
>
> – Ottawa Mayor Larry O'Brien

to the Trans Canada in the south, plus a north-eastern highway connecting Montreal to North Bay and the northern Trans Canada route.

COMING AND GOING

Distances to Ottawa from other major points in Canada:
- Vancouver: 4,600 km
- Calgary: 3,550 km
- Toronto: 450 km
- Montreal: 200 km
- Halifax: 1,450 km
- St. John's: 2,800 km

To reach Ottawa from some other major cities around the world:
- Tokyo: 10,345 km
- Paris: 5,663 km
- London: 5,376 km
- Miami: 2,217 km
- Chicago: 1,047 km
- New York: 546 km

Source: Go Canada.

Did you know...

> ... that Ottawa's 2008-2009 bus strike was longest running bus strike to date, and has cost taxpayers over $13.4 million?

Did you know...

> ...that Ottawa has maintained one of the lowest unemployment rates in all of Canada, even as the city's population grew 58 per cent in the last 25 years?

CONSTRUCTION

The city of Ottawa issued $83.4 million non- residential building permits in the early part of 2016. Permits issued in June 2016 included $92.9 million in non-residential permits which is up 35.9 percent from June 2015. Non-residential construction in Ottawa is expected to continue fueling economic growth in the coming years. Construction of the Confederation Line-the largest infrastructure investment project in Ottawa to date at $2.1 billion, is underway. The Province of Ontario has committed $1.16 billion towards the Stage 2 light Rail Transit initiative which is believed will support the momentum in the construction sector past 2018.

FARMIN' IN THE CITY

Ottawa is the largest farming city in Canada, and is characterized by thriving and technologically advanced dairy, beef, pork, poultry and cash-crop sectors. Known for its diversity, Ottawa is home to many niche operations including, but not limited to, apiaries, berries, Christmas trees, emus, greenhouse businesses, horse farms, organic farms and vegetables.

Ottawa's 1,492 farms create jobs for over 50,000 labourers and bring in over $400 million each year. The capital value of the land and equipment is more than $1 billion.

ECONOMY

Take 5 OTTAWA'S TOP FIVE AGRICULTURAL PRODUCTS

1. *Dairy*
2. *Beef cattle*
3. *Vegetables*
4. *Field crops*
5. *Grain and oilseed, excluding wheat*

Source: City of Ottawa.

TECHNOLOGY OUTLOOK

- Employment in the sector is dropping, down almost 2,800 jobs since 2008, registering 75,132 jobs by the end of 2016.
- Venture capital investment, which hit a high of $1.3 billion in 2000, was only $130.2 million in 2008, down from $184.5 million in 2007. However, 2015 saw a renewal with several major high-tech players, including Corsa, GAN Systems. You.I labs and Grafoid investing multi-millions of dollars. The venture capital doubled that year from 2014, topping out at $142,000,000.

Source: OCRI.

Did you know...

. . . that the present site of the Parliament Buildings and much of downtown Ottawa was originally part of a 200-acre plot purchased in 1821 for 95 pounds by Nicholas Sparks, a thrifty farmhand who worked for Philemon Wright? The land is now assessed at over $100 million.

Did you know...

. . . that Ottawa's agricultural revenue, drawn from over 1,300 farms, is greater than that of Toronto, Montreal, Vancouver, Edmonton and Calgary combined? More than 40 percent of rural Ottawa is producing farmland, some 115,806 hectares.

Take 5: OTTAWA'S TOP FIVE COMPETITORS FOR HIGH TECHNOLOGY COMPANIES LOOKING TO RELOCATE:

1. Raleigh-Durham, North Carolina
2. San Jose, California
3. Orange County, California
4. Austin, Texas
5. Boulder, Colorado

Source: City of Ottawa

BOSS O'BRIEN

In September 2016, Calian Technologies Ltd. of Ottawa posted $242 million in total revenue for 2015, more than any other fiscal year. There are currently over 2,700 employees. When it started in 1982, Calian Technologies was a one-man operation—an Ottawa native son named Larry O'Brien—who had just bounced out of owning a company that had gone bankrupt.

In early 2005, O'Brien retired as Calian's CEO, though he continued on the Board of Directors. By then he had grown Calian to the point it comfortably acquired SED Systems, moving with that beyond consultation to system design and operation with a focus on aerospace. He also guided the company over the rocky road from being privately held to a public company. Presumably, O'Brien should have then said his thank-you's for a great run and taken a break.

He didn't. Instead, he stepped into the municipal political arena and, in November 2006, he was elected Mayor of Ottawa.

Did you know...

... that Ottawa brings in over $1.1 billion annually due to tourism and conventions?

ECONOMY

Did you know...

... that there are more than 1,800 high technology companies in Ottawa? Ottawa's high tech sector set an all-time high for employees with 68,000 people at 1,800 companies
Source: Ottawa Business Journal March 2016

INNOVATION

The Innovation Centre at Bayview Yards was built off an initial $30 million from the City of Ottawa and smart, collaborative partnerships. Key programs that the Center will launch will be a Global Cybersecurity Program and a makerspace and digital media lab. In June 2016, FedDEv Ontario announced an $8 million contribution to the Innovation Centre at Bayview Yards for new programming and technology. The city hopes this will be the beginning of the creation of a technology hub.

The Innovation Center officially opened in November 2016.

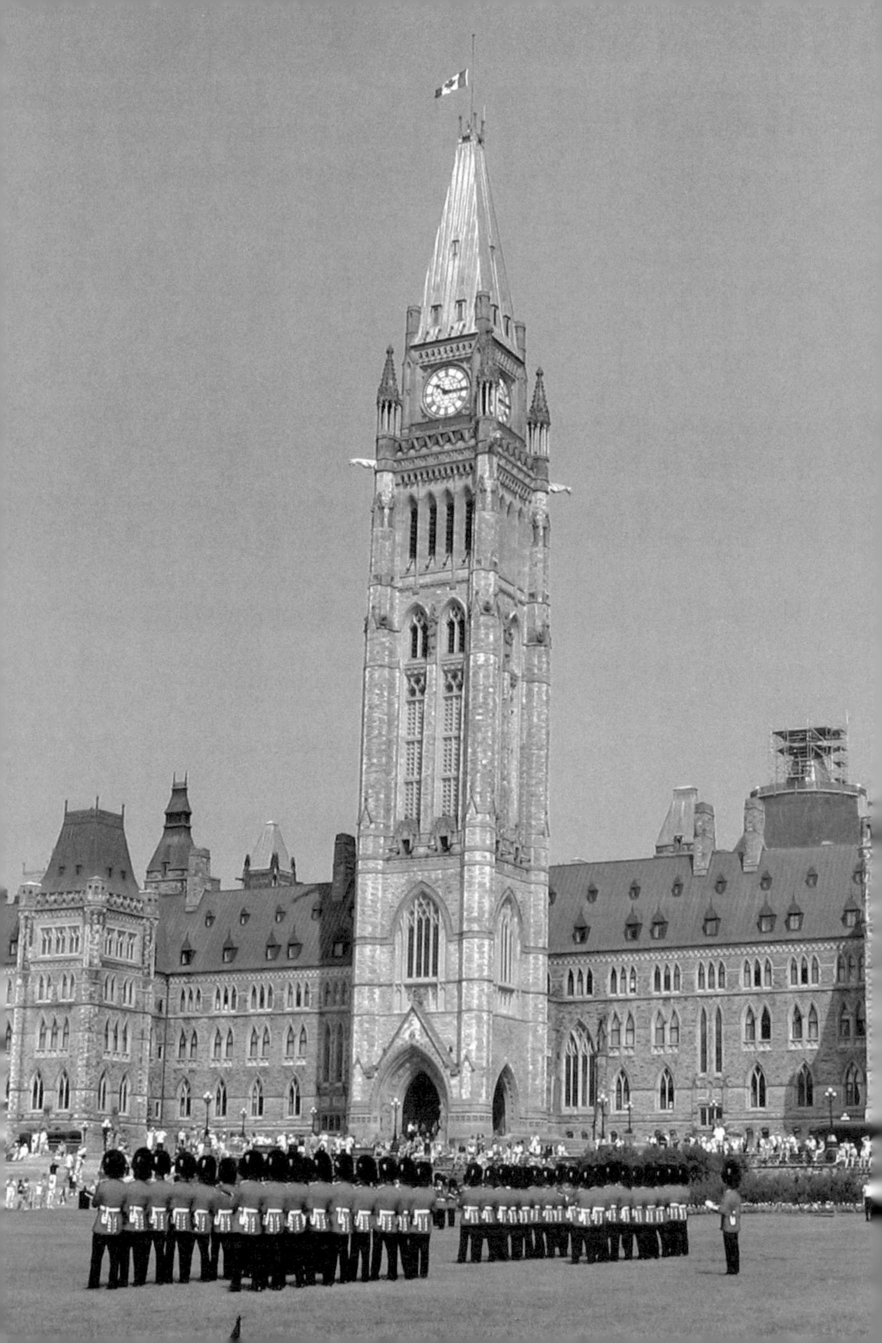

POLITICS

Politics

Cynics might say that Ottawa represents the most perfect of political storms. Municipal government mixes with a significant provincial government presence in a city that is the nation's capital. Politics in Ottawa is not an elective you take at university, it is an industry.

CITY GOVERNMENT
The city of Ottawa is governed by an elected 24-member city council comprised of 23 councilors, representing the city's individual wards. The mayor and city councilors serve four-year terms, with the next municipal election scheduled for November, 2018.

STANDING COMMITTEES
City council appoints standing committees, made up solely of councillors, to study specific issues before bringing them to a meeting of city council. There are 16 advisory committees which provide advice to city council and staff on specifically mandated areas of interest, and contribute to the development of policies, programs and initiatives. Advisory committees are composed of volunteers, appointed by council.

MEET THE OTHER PLAYERS

Ottawa is unique among cities of Canada because it is the country's capital.

Most cities have elected municipal officials with the power to shape the industry, culture and character of their city. Roads, sewers, bridges, land development, policing, public health, snow removal, parks and recreation are among the traditional jurisdictions of city government. Not entirely so in Ottawa.

Ottawa has two other players: the federal government and a crown corporation, the National Capital Commission. To be effective, members of Ottawa's city council must sometimes be as nimble-witted as sand salesmen in the Sahara Desert.

First off, the National Capital Commission owns more than 10 percent of the city's land area, including the Greenbelt, considerable rural agricultural land, museum and heritage properties, and some residential land. Moreover, none of this is subject to the city's planning and development processes. The size of the commission's holdings makes it a heavy hitter at any planning session city council undertakes, yet not a member of the commission is elected. Ottawa's commercial real estate market is dominated by federal government needs. The government dictates where they want their offices. Retail and service industry supports must follow.

Take 5 TOP FIVE QUOTES
FROM THE WHITTON WIT

1. "Whatever women do, they must do twice as well as men to be thought half as good. Luckily, this is not difficult."
2. "Man cannot live by incompetence alone."
3. "When one must, one can."
4. "It's how you deal with failure that determines how you achieve success."
5. "We never reflect how pleasant it is to ask for nothing."

POLITICS

POLITICAL NUMBERS
- Number of federal ridings in Ottawa: 5 of 336
- Number of provincial ridings in Ottawa: 8 of 122
- Representation, federal: two cabinet ministers
- Representation, provincial: premier plus two cabinet ministers
- City Council: Mayor plus 23 members

UNELECTED OFFICIALS, OTHER THAN THOSE ON COMMITTEES AND ADVISORY BOARDS
- Senate: 105
- National Capital Commission: 16
- The diplomatic corps: 130 embassies, consulates, high commissions
- Registered lobbyists: 8,500

Source: Parliament of Canada.

OPERATING BUDGET

The 2016 operating budget for the City of Ottawa is based on $3.6 billion in revenue, obtained from these sources:
- Property Taxes: $1.4 billion
- Federal/Provincial Subsidies: $550 million
- User Fees: $500 million
- Water/Sewer Rates: $215 million
- Payments in lieu of Taxes: $192 million
- Investment income: $43 million

Where the money is spent is somewhat more difficult to determine. Broken down, it looks like this:
- Compensation: $1,543,604
- Transfers/Grants/Other: $1,112,129
- Materials and services: $568,698
- Materials and Supplies: 8 percent
- Other internal: $130,000

Did you know...

... that 31 of Bytown and Ottawa's 58 ex-mayors are buried in Ottawa's 152-year old Beechwood Cemetery? It is officially designated as Canada's National Cemetery.

HIGH COST OF GOVERNMENT

In 2016, it cost the city of Ottawa $3.2 billion to operate. The biggest single expenses was transit, which totaled more than $530 million. Second on the list is employment and financial assistance.

Here's where another large portion was spent:

- Policing: $260 million
- Fleet services: $300 million
- Social housing: $101 million
- Surface operations: $122.1 million
- Fire: $154.8 million
- Child care: $111 million
- Parks and recreation: $164 million
- Paramedic services: $85.6 million
- City manager's office: $62 million
- Solid services: $5,230 million
- Long term care: $62.2 million
- Health: $59 million
- Information technology services: $62.8 million
- Traffic and parking: $48.7 million
- Libraries: $49.2 million
- By-law services: $18 million

Did you know...

... that the city of Ottawa is a complex service delivery organization with approximately 12,000 employees, and is responsible for managing more than $26 billion in public assets?

POLITICS

They Said It

> "The art of politics is learning to walk with your back to the wall, your elbows high, and a smile on your face."
>
> – Jean Chretien, 1985

LONG SERVING
Ottawa's longest serving mayor was J.E. Stanley Lewis, who held office from 1936 to 1948. The next two longest serving mayors were Charlotte Whitton (1951-56 and 1961-64) and Marion Dewar (1978-85).

CITY DEBT
Ottawa's total debt currently stands at 1.7 billion.

PROPERTY TAXES
Based on a sample house as defined as a 25 to 30 year-old detached 3-bedroom bungalow with a main floor area of 1,200 square feet, finished full basement and a double car garage, on a 6,000 square foot lot. Utility charges include telephones, power, water, sewer, land drainage and garbage collection.

AVERAGE PROPERTY TAXES

Toronto	$3,947
Ottawa	**$4,057**
Saskatoon	$4,400
Vancouver	$2,322
Regina	$4,065
Edmonton	$2,947
Halifax	$3,283
Calgary	$3,973
Montreal	$2,704
Winnipeg	$3,529

Source: City of Edmonton 2007 Study.

Ottawa Mayors

Term	Name	Profession
BYTOWN		
John Scott	1847	Lawyer
John Bower Lewis	1848	Lawyer
Robert Hervey	1849	Lawyer
John Scott	1850	Lawyer
Charles Sparrow	1851	Tanner and general store
R. W. Scott	1852	Lawyer
J. B. Turgeon	1853	Educator
Henry J. Friel	1854	Journalist
BYTOWN BECOMES OTTAWA		
John Bower Lewis	1855 – 1857	Lawyer
Edward MacGillivray	1858 – 1859	Fur trader and General store
Alexander Workman	1860 – 1862	Hardware business
Henry J. Friel	1863	Journalist
M. K. Dickinson	1864 – 1866	Sawmill and grist mill owner
Robert Lyon	1867	Lawyer
Henry J. Friel	1868 – 1869	Journalist
John Rochester	1870 – 1871	Sawmill operator
Eugene Martineau	1872 – 1873	Businessman
J. P. Featherston	1874 – 1875	Druggist
G. B. Lyon-Fellowes	1876	Unknown
William Henry Waller	1877	Journalist and insurance broker
C. W. Bangs	1878	Businessman and hotelier
Charles H. MacIntosh	1879 – 1881	Journalist
Pierre St. Jean, M.D.	1882 – 1883	Doctor
C. T. Bate	1884	Grocer and banker
Francis MacDougal	1885 – 1886	Businessman
McLeod Stewart	1887 – 1888	Lawyer
Jacob Erratt	1889 – 1890	Businessman
Thomas Bitkett	1891	Businessman
Olivier Durocher	1892 – 1893	Shoemaker
George Cox	1894	Unknown
William Borthwick	1895 – 1896	Timber trade and grocer
Samuel Bingham	1897 – 1898	Logger and businessman
Thomas Payment	1899 – 1900	Bookkeeper and pharmacist
W. D. Morris	1901	Businessman
James Davidson	1901	Businessman
Fred Cook	1902 – 1903	Journalist
James A. Ellis	1904 – 1906	Unknown

POLITICS

Term	Name	Profession
Robert Hastey	1906	Stagecoach business
D'Arcy Scott	1907 – 1908	Lawyer
Napoleon Champagne	1908	Lawyer
Charles Hopewell	1909 – 1912	Magistrate
Edward H. Hinchey	1912	Federal employee
James A. Ellis	1913	Unknown
Taylor McVeity	1914	Lawyer
Nelson D. Porter	1915 – 1916	Insurance and real estate
Harold Fisher	1917 – 1920	Lawyer
Frank H. Plant	1921 – 1923	Alderman
Henry Watters	1924	Pharmacist
Napoleon Champagne	1924	Lawyer
John P. Balharrie	1925 – 1927	Real Estate
Arthur Ellis	1928 – 1929	Lawyer
Frank H. Plant	1930	Alderman
John J. Allen	1931 – 1933	Pharmacist, broker
Patrick Nolan	1934 – 1935	Pharmacist, movie theatre owner
J. E. Stanley Lewis	1936 – 1948	Electrical store owner
E. A. Bourque	1949 – 1950	Business man
Grenville Goodwin	1951	Optometrist
Charlotte Whitton	1951 – 1956	Canadian Council on Social Development Director
George H. Nelms	1957 – 1960	Optician
Charlotte Whitton	1961 – 1964	Canadian Council on Social Development Director
Donald Bartlett Reid	1965 – 1969	Businessman
Kenneth H. Fogarty, Q.C.	1970 – 1972	Lawyer
Pierre Benoit	1972 – 1974	Lawyer
Lorry Greenberg	1975 – 1978	Business man
Marion Dewar	1978 – 1985	Public Health nurse
James Durrell	1985 – 1991	Insurance executive
Marc LaViolette	1991	High school teacher
Jacquelin Holzman	1991 – 1997	Volunteer
Jim Watson	1997 – 2000	Journalist
Allen Higden (Acting)	2000 – 2001	Teacher and Analyst

POST AMALGAMATION

Bob Chiarelli	2001 – 2006	Lawyer and business man
Larry O'Brien	2006 – 2010	Information Technologist
Jim Watson	2010 – present	Public servant

Did you know...

...that the city of Ottawa has had three women mayors? Toronto has had only two while Montreal, Calgary and Vancouver have had none.

POLITICAL FIRSTS: WOMEN IN OTTAWA

1884: Women earn the municipal franchise

1917: Women earn the provincial franchise

1918: Ottawa women first cast federal votes

1921: First woman MP, Anges Macphail

1930: First woman senator, CairineWilson

1951: First female mayor of Ottawa (and of a Canadian city), Charlotte Whitton

1957: First woman federal cabinet minister, Ellen Fairclough

1980: First female speaker in the House of Commons, Jeanne Sauvé

1984: First female Governor General, Jeanne Sauvé

1989: First woman to head a federal party: Audrey McLaughlin

1993: First female Prime Minister, Kim Campbell

1993: First woman deputy Prime Minister, Sheila Copps

2000: First female leader of the Opposition in the House of Commons, Deborah Gray.

2006: Jack Layton's New Democratic Caucus is 43% female.

2007: First woman to serve as leader of the Opposition in the Senate, Celine Hervieux-Payette.

2015: First gender-balanced Cabinet introduced by Prime Minister Justin Trudeau.

2016: First time women make up 30% of the Senate.

Did you know...

...that in 2001, when Ottawa was amalgamated to include 11 other municipalities, 4 of these municipalities had female mayors?

POLITICS

Lady Charlotte

Love her or hate her, no one can deny that Charlotte Whitton remains one of the most interesting, controversial and fiery personalities in the history of Ottawa politics.

After an academic career at Queens, Whitton spent the 1920s crusading on behalf of children. She fought for better standards in the care of juvenile immigrants and neglected children. In 1920, she became director of the Canadian Council on Child Welfare.

During the Great Depression, Whitton became a key federal adviser on unemployment relief to the government. The socially conservative Whitton, however, was not a popular figure for opposing spending on the unemployed.

After resigning from the Child Welfare Council in 1941, Whitton took up the cause of the role of women in politics and the workplace. Once again, though, Whitton's position was problematic. Not only did she oppose more liberal divorce laws, but she was against working women. Women, she felt, belonged in the home.

Still, Whitton had her supporters, especially among women. In 1950, Charlotte Whitton was elected Mayor of Ottawa. In doing so, Whitton became the first female mayor in Canada. A record number of people turned out to vote and many credit Whitton for the turnout. Whitton would end up serving the city as mayor from 1951-1956 and from 1961-1964. She returned to council as alderman from 1967-1972.

Whitton's terms as mayor were, not surprisingly, riddled with controversy. During a heated Board of Control meeting, Whitton pulled out a cap gun and aimed it at one of the controllers. At another meeting, The *Globe and Mail* reported that Whitton had thrashed a fellow controller "with her fists."

As the CBC reported in Whitton's 1975 obituary: "[She] carved her noisy way into the male dominated world of politics. Once there, she shouted, joked, cajoled, titillated and annoyed in all directions." Her election led to national fame, but it was her energetic and peppery personality that keeps her name well known.

Did you know...

> ... that the Arthur Ellis, who was Ottawa's mayor during 1928 and 1929 was not Arthur Ellis, Canada's official hangman? The real name of the hangman was Arthur English and he came from a long line of professional hangmen going back 300 years. Mayor Ellis was a lawyer who went on to sit in the Ontario legislature until 1937.

KEEPING IT IN THE FAMILY

Politics in Canada has often been a family affair. Ex-Prime Minister Paul Martin's father was a former federal cabinet minister. Jean Chretien's father was a veteran political organizer. Sheila Copps' father was the former mayor of Hamilton. Also, Prime Minister Justin Trudeau's father was the late Prime Minister Pierre Elliott Trudeau.

The reigning political family in Canada has to be Ottawa's own McGuinty's. The father, Dalton Senior, was a Liberal MPP from Ottawa South. His son, Dalton Junior, inherited the Ottawa South provincial seat and went on to become Premier of Ontario. Not to be outdone, another son, David, was elected Member of Parliament, also for Ottawa South.

In these cases, and in most since Confederation, the relatives follow party lines, apples never falling far from the tree. But the family that campaigns together may not always stay together, that is, not in the same party. Robert Layton was twice elected to the House of Commons waving the Progressive Conservative banner. His son, Jack, is also a Member of Parliament. But forget the Tories. Jack is currently the Leader of the New Democratic Party. The Layton tree seems to have been perched on top of a steep hill.

POLITICS

Did you know...

> ... that Gatineau Park is the only park in Canada outside the jurisdiction of Parks Canada? The Gatineau Park is owned and operated by the National Capital Commission.

STATUES ON PARLIAMENT HILL

The following people have been immortalized in sculpture on Parliament Hill: Sir George-Étienne Cartier, Sir John A. Macdonald, Sir Louis-Hippolyte Lafontaine, Lester B. Pearson, Queen Victoria, George Brown, Alexander Mackenzie, Thomas D'Arcy McGee, Robert Baldwin, Queen Elizabeth, Persons Case Women (the Famous Five: Henrietta Muir Edward, Emily Murphy, Louise McKinney, Nellie McClung and Irene Parlby), William Lyon Mackenzie King, Sir Wilfrid Laurier, John Diefenbaker and Sir Robert Borden.

VOTER TURNOUTS

Although the weather was good and skies sunny, the 2014 municipal election voter turnout was low, at just 39.7 percent of eligible voters. This is equal to about four out of ten voters. Mayor Jim Watson was a strong favorite and ran away with the race. Because there was no strong mayoral race, it is speculated that people may just not have been excited about getting out to vote.

Source: City of Ottawa.

Did you know...

> ... that provided advance notice is given to authorities and a mutually agreed time is scheduled, demonstrations of well-controlled civil disobedience are permitted on Parliament Hill?

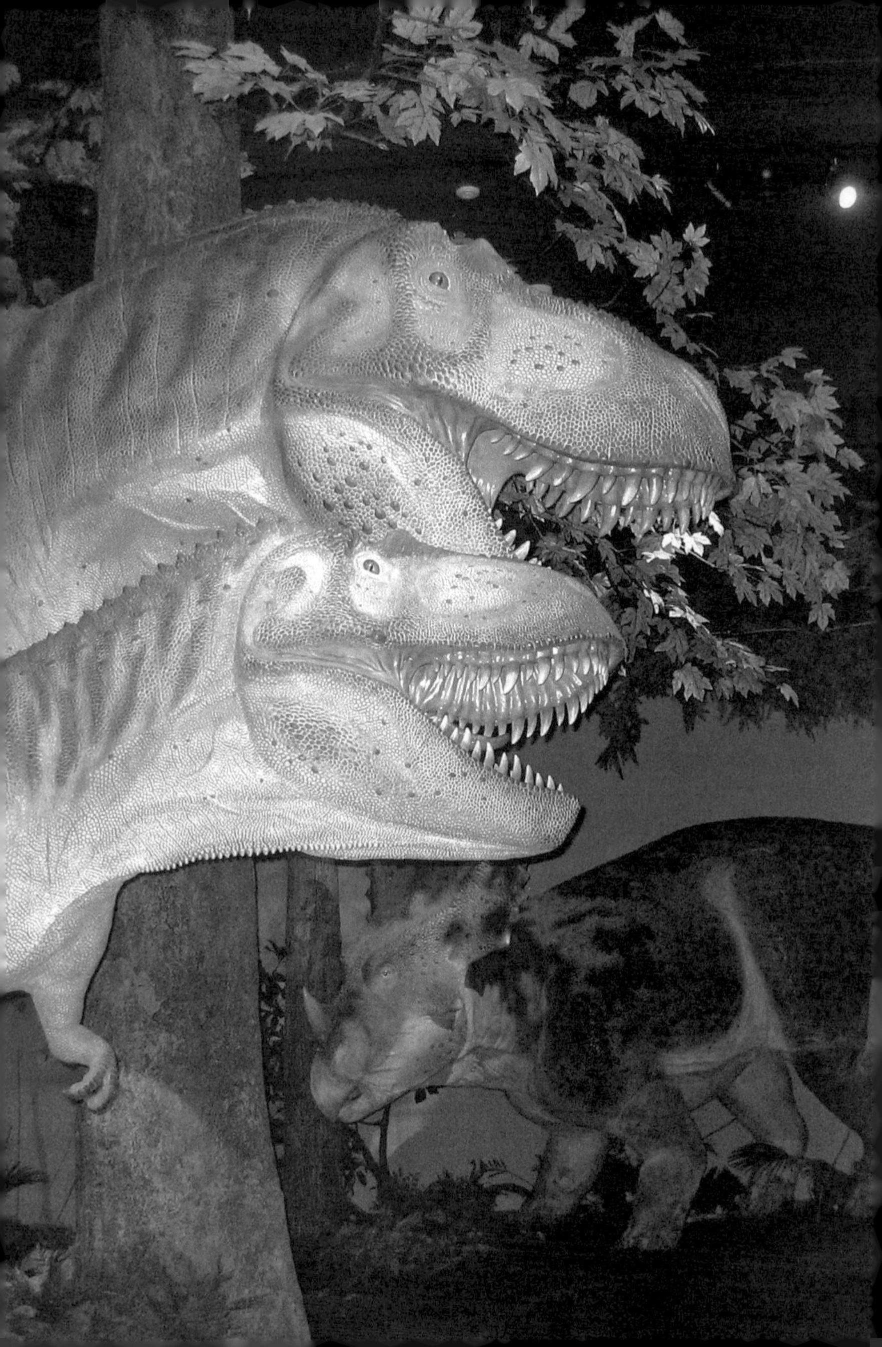

THEN AND NOW

Then and Now

When France's ambitions in North America came to an end in 1759, the Ottawa area came under British rule and in short order, settlers from the United States began to stake claims to the land. The next major development in the history of the city came after the War of 1812. Great Britain was becoming increasingly convinced that the U.S. had designs on their possessions, namely present day Canada.

Great Britain had decisions to make. It chose Ottawa as the new capital, not because it was the most dynamic choice but rather because it was the furthest away from the United States. In the period of just over 100 years Ottawa moved from a distant unpopulated outpost to lumber town to nation's capital. It has been an extraordinary transition, and transition has been a central theme in the *history of the city*.

They Said It

> "*The city is located in the middle of nowhere, and the nowhere is quite attractive.*"
>
> – John Ibbitson, Globe and Mail

POPULATION THEN AND NOW

1901	101,102
1921	152,868
1941	206,367
1961	358,410
1981	546,850
2006	812,129
2015:	883,391
2017:	960,000

Source: Statistics Canada.

GENDER (IM)BALANCE

Year	Men	Women
1901:	27,442	30,198
1921:	50,245	57,298
1931:	59,183	67,689
1941:	72,600	82,351
1951:	94,629	107,416
1961:	129,035	139,171
1971:	145,315	157,030
1981:	137,865	153,985
2016:	450,650	509,350

Source: Ottawa An Illustrated History.

ETHNIC ORIGIN OF OTTAWA'S POPULATION

Individuals were able to choose more than one response.

Canadian: 28.4%
French: 21.5%
English: 24.3%
Irish: 22.5%
Scottish: 19.8%
German: 8.4%
Italian: 4.9%

THEN AND NOW

DEPRESSION FREE

Ottawa was among the very few places to escape the ravages of the Great Depression. It seems counter-intuitive, but because the country was grappling with one of the great upheavals of the last hundred years, the city was actually busier than it might normally be.

From 1929-1932, it was mostly business as usual in Ottawa. It was only after the new National Research Council building was completed that government work slowed down. Even then the government laid off very few people. Other civil servants had to take pay cuts, but with the cost of living decreasing, life was still manageable.

Even during the worst years of the depression in Ottawa, between 1932-35, the most destitute people were not locals but transients who had come to town in search of work.

TRAINS TO NOWHERE

Ottawa's first train station annoyed just about everybody. Built in 1895, many people complained that it was little more than a personal depot for its owner, J.R. Booth. As one writer noted in a 1904 Ottawa Citizen piece: "The present so-called depot wouldn't be acceptable as a lobster packing warehouse."

The city got its first 'real' train station in 1912, when Grand Trunk Railway built the dazzling Union Station (built in Classic Revival style) and the adjacent luxury hotel, the Château Laurier. Together, the buildings gave the old lumber town a touch of class.

As beautiful as it may have been, Union Station's train traffic was a hindrance to the city's growth. As early as 1915, there were 11 individual railway lines in Ottawa and 150 crossings, creating a traffic nightmare. In the late 1940s it was recommended the train station be moved away from downtown.

Did you know...

... that in 1927 Ottawa city council approved the installation of Canada's first automatic traffic light system?

In 1966, they did just that. Tracks were torn up to create parks, parkways and highways, and a new Ottawa Train Station was opened in the city's east end. Initially, Union Station was to be demolished, but when Ottawans protested the building was kept alive. Although the building is closed to the public, it is living on as a conference centre for the Canadian government.

Lords of Lumber

Ottawa owes much to Americans. Philemon Wright, a canny New Englander, arrived here in 1800. Although he left Massachusetts under a darkening cloud of bad debt and allegations of theft, here he secured a substantial land grant and had with him a contingent of five families and thirty labourers to make the best of it.

He settled what is now Gatineau (Hull), reasoning that where white pine grew in abundance, so, too, would crops. He named his settlement Wrightsville and was regarded as a "benevolent autocrat" by his citizenry.

In 1806, he shipped the first timber raft to Montreal. In effect, he showed the way, though decades would pass before the northern Ottawa Valley's riches of white pine were fully realized by enterprising businessmen.

Henry Bronson arrived in nearby Bytown from New York State in 1848, after badgering his New York partners to finally look northward to the Ottawa Valley's forests.

In 1852, having won them over, and having secured deals to draw power from the Chaudiere Falls, Bronson's sawmill business took off. The 1854-66 Reciprocity Treaty, providing for duty free, sawn lumber exports, consolidated his success. Bronson's lumber operations were soon grossing more than $1 million annually.

While Wright and Bronson could certainly take places at the head table of Ottawa Valley's timber barons, the podium belongs to John R. Booth. Though he was born in rural Quebec where he learned lumber jacking, Booth's real education came in Vermont,

THEN AND NOW

TRANSIT

The history of public transit in Ottawa goes back to Confederation. In 1866, the Ottawa City Passenger Railway Company began using horse-drawn trolleys, and in 1891 the company merged into the Ottawa Electric Street Railway Company and began operating electric trolleys. In its first year, the trolleys carried more than 1.5 million passengers and by 1895 it was carrying more than four million passengers a year. While buses first appeared in 1924, trolleys remained the primary mode of public transit until 1959.

---

where he learned sawmilling and business.

In 1859, Booth was 32 years old when his big break came. He won the contract to supply lumber for construction of the Parliament Buildings. By 1865 his mills were turning out eight million board feet of sawn lumber. In 1870 he had 2,000 mill workers and another 4,000 workers in his forests. By 1890, he had the highest daily output in the world.

Booth was not content to simply cut, saw, and sell lumber. He had interests in shipping and railroads. Only after he died did his son and heir discover that Booth owned a small fleet of Great Lakes freighters primarily involved in grain transport.

E.B. Eddy, a Vermonter, arrived in Hull in 1851, just when Hull's economy was stagnating, primarily due to Philemon Wright's propensity to discourage competition. Eddy started out by manufacturing sulphur matches. Soon he diversified into manufacturing wooden washboards, clothespins and pails.

With his business expanding, he established a sawmill and factories on the Hull side of the Chaudiere Falls. By the turn of the century, Eddy's company was the largest match manufacturer in the British Empire. His sawmills turned out 75 million board feet a year. The match king had also branched out into the pulp and paper business. By then, he was carrying the largest payroll in Hull. Twice his factories were nearly wiped out by fire. Twice he rebuilt, coming back bigger and stronger than before.

Did you know...

> ... that Ottawa's ByWard Market was established in 1826 and is the oldest running market in Canada?

In 1972, the Ottawa-Carleton Regional Transit Commission (which Ottawans call OC Transpo) was created. Bus service was extended into neighbourhoods and exclusive bus lanes were introduced.

One of the unique features of Ottawa's transit system is the Transitway. The Transitway consists of 31 km of bus-only roads that provide a fast and effective link for Ottawa urban areas.

In 2001, years after turning their back on rail service, Ottawa's city planners decided to introduce the O-Train, a light rail transit service. There are plans to expand the O-Train to include downtown, connect East-West suburbs and provide service to the airport.

PLANES, PAST AND PRESENT

In the 1920s, there were few planes in Canada, and most of those that were in Canada were in the Ottawa area and owned by the Royal Canadian Air Force at their base in the Rockcliffe area.

On the south side of the city was a strip of land used by Charles Lindbergh during his flight. Except for Lindbergh's visit, the land went unused until the Ottawa Flying Club started up in 1928.

When the owners of the land were unable to pay its rent, one of the flying club members, A. Barnet MacLaren, bought the land. While MacLaren wanted to help out his buddies at the club, he also had another reason: he had just formed Laurentian Air Services and needed an airport.

Did you know...

> ... that in 1892 Ottawa entrepreneur Thomas Ahearn became the first person in the world to make a meal using electricity?

THEN AND NOW

A Capital Controversy

Then as now, Ottawa gets little respect or acknowledgment as Canada's capital. Ask most Americans and they'll tell you Toronto is the capital. It wasn't much different back in 1857 when Queen Victoria first named Ottawa as the new capital.

Debates about the location of the capital date back to 1841 when the Province of Canada was formed as part of the Act of Union. Quebec and Toronto were deemed too far to the east and west, respectively. Kingston was initially selected by the Governor General, but when he died the capital was switched to Montreal. That move lasted only five years. During the Rebellion Losses Act of 1849, Parliament was burned down.

The government then decided to rotate the location of the capital between Toronto and Quebec. This dubious experiment lasted a few short years until it was decided that it was an inconvenient and expensive process.

Finally, Governor General Head used his. He asked Queen Victoria to sort things out once and for all.

Ottawa quickly became the most logical option. Selecting Quebec, it was felt, would anger Canada West. Choosing Toronto would irk everyone else. Kingston was called "a dead place" and Montreal was too unpredictable.

While some objected that Ottawa was just a wild, lumber town, Governor General Head felt that Ottawa was ideally situated for defense because of its distance from the American border. In the end, though, Head told Queen Victoria frankly that she had "a choice of evils, and the least evil will, I think, be Ottawa."

On January 30, 1858, the *Ottawa Tribune* published the Queen's decision:

"Ottawa has been selected by her Majesty as the capital of Canada. . . Ottawa is now destined to advance with rapid strides on the road to prosperity. Her natural advantages will be brought prominently before the country, and the time is not far distant when she will rank as one of the first-rate cities of Canada." And to this day, not a day goes by that a rumbling over Victoria's decision can't be heard somewhere in Canada.

They Said It

> "Bytown had 10,000 lumbermen – 8,000 of them drunks."
> – Attributed to former **Ottawa Mayor Charlotte Whitton**

MacLaren held the land for just two years before selling it off to the Federal Government. The newly renamed Ottawa Airport officially opened in August 1938 with Trans-Canada Airlines operating regular service throughout Canada.

In 1950, the airport underwent its first major expansion to accommodate the emergence of jet aircraft. After many delays, the new terminal was finally opened in 1960. In 1997, the airport was renamed Macdonald-Cartier Airport (after John A. Macdonald and Georges-Etienne Cartier).

On October 12, 2003, a new state-of-the-art, 650,000 square foot Passenger Terminal Building opened for business. The new airport terminal is a small marvel compared to the cramped and dingy old terminal. Natural light beams through a more spacey and calm terminal. How zen is it? As passengers take the escalator down to the arrival area, they are greeted by the calm sounds of a waterfall. In 2008, twelve additional gates and seven jetways were opened.

Did you know...

... that after Charles Lindbergh's flight to Ottawa in his famous *Spirit of St. Louis*, one of the accompanying pursuit planes crashed, killing the pilot? During a funeral a few days later, Lindbergh made a series of low-level passes over the funeral and dropped flowers.

THEN AND NOW

Bio CANADA'S THOMAS EDISON

One of Ottawa's early entrepreneurs was Thomas Ahearn. In 1877, Ahearn devised a rudimentary telephone system using two homemade cigar boxes, magnets and wire. Using existing telegraph lines, Ahearn set up a routing from Pembroke to Ottawa, making Ottawa's first long-distance telephone call. One Alexander Graham Bell was not amused and threatened Ahearn with legal action. In the end, though, Bell was shrewd. He appointed Ahearn as manager of Bell Telegraphone Company's Ottawa office.

In 1881, Ahearn partnered with Warren Soper to open an electrical contracting firm on Sparks Street (the building still exists today). The company built long-distance lines for Bell Telephone Company in Pembroke, Montreal and Quebec. In 1882, the duo constructed a power station on the Ottawa River and introduced electric light to Ottawa. In 1897, the company was hired to light up Parliament Hill for Queen Victoria's Diamond Jubilee. That same year, they entertained Ottawa children by dressing up as Santa and decorating a streetcar with lights.

In 1891, Ahearn and Soper established yet another company, the Ottawa Electric Railway, and replaced horse-drawn streetcars with electric ones. On June 29, 1891, Ahearn was behind the wheel of the first car as thousands of people looked on with amazement. To keep things toasty during Ottawa's harsh winters, Ahearn ran electrically-heated water under the floor of the cars. He also invented a rotating brush cleaner to keep the tracks clear of snow.

In 1892, Ahearn became the first person in the world to make a meal using electricity. Ahearn and his colleagues prepared an elaborate meal in an electric car shed on Albert St., then brought the items by car to the elegant Windsor Hotel at Queen and Metcalfe. After sampling the meal, the Hotel's manager immediately ordered one of Ahearn's ovens.

HORSELESS CARRIAGE

Canada's first self-propelled automobile is alive and well and staying in Ottawa. The steam-powered vehicle was invented in the mid-1860s by Quebec watchmaker Henry Seth Taylor; after crashing the vehicle, Taylor put the remains in a barn in Stanstead Plain, Quebec. They were later sold to an American who rebuilt the vehicle. In 1984, the vehicle was acquired by the Canada Science and Technology Museum in Ottawa, where it is on display from time to time.

OTTAWA'S TITANIC CONNECTION

It seems that every city has a connection to the Titanic tragedy. Ottawa is no exception. One of its victims was Charles Melville Hays, president of the Grand Trunk Railway that commissioned the construction of a luxurious new hotel called the Fairmont Château Laurier to be built in a 16th century French Château style across from the new railway station.

Despite some disagreements and budget cuts, the hotel was on schedule for its grand opening on April 26, 1912. Hays, though, would not be there. On his return to Canada with dining room furniture for his new hotel, Hays perished aboard the Titanic. When news reached Ottawa of Hays' death, the opening ceremony was cancelled. The hotel would eventually open that June. In a subdued opening, Wilfred Laurier simply signed the registry as the hotel's first guest.

Although Hays never lived to see the hotel, the Fairmont Château Laurier remains one of the most recognizable buildings in Ottawa and was a key turning point in helping Ottawa shift from a rough and tumble lumber town to a modern metropolis.

Did you know...

. . . that Ottawa's F.C.P. Henroteau patented the Television Camera in 1934?

THEN AND NOW

CANADA HITS THE SILVER SCREEN

Thanks to the initiative of two brothers, Ottawa was the first Canadian city to experience the lights and shadows of moving pictures.

George and Andrew Holland were young entrepreneurs with a passion for technology and invention. While working for Thomas Edison's company, they introduced Canada to the typewriter and phonograph.

Edison was so impressed with the brothers' marketing success that in 1894 he asked them to exhibit his new kinetoscope (a moving picture machine) in New York in the world's first Kinetoscope parlour. For a nickel, people could peer into the viewfinder at the top of the machine and watch short moving pictures.

A few months later the brothers brought the invention home to Ottawa and set up a parlour on the ground floor of a building on Sparks Street. On November 3, 1894, Ottawa became the first Canadian city to experience the magic of moving pictures. There was no sound or story, but the images of boxing matches and saucy dancing burlesque girls were more than enough to dazzle the peeping Ottawa public.

A few years later, they took the moving image experience a step further when they were called upon by Edison to promote his new motion picture machine called the Vitascope. On July 21, 1896, Ottawans gathered under a tent at what is now the intersection of Holland Avenue and Ruskin Street to witness the debut of the silver screen in Canada.

OVERDUE

With new and used bookstores, the National Library and Archives, Writer's Festival and a bevy of branches of the Ottawa Public Library, Ottawa today is a literary delight.

Did you know...

... that the creation of the Stanley Cup was first announced in 1892 during a dinner of the Ottawa Amateur Athletic Association?

Prior to the 20th century, however, outside of a few hotel lobby reading rooms and some fee-based libraries, there literally was no place for anyone to read. That all changed when the Local Council of Women pushed for and secured a building. When the city voted down the idea saying they didn't have money for such a luxury, the women sought outside help.

In 1901, a letter for financial help was sent to the American steel baron, Andrew Carnegie. Carnegie had already funded over 3,000 libraries around the world and agreed to give the city $100,000 to build a library and $7,500 a year to maintain the building if it provided the site.

It took city council two years to accept Carnegie's offer. On April 30, 1906, Ottawa's first public library was officially opened. It was located at the corner of Metcalfe and Laurier Avenue West (where the present Main Branch of the Ottawa Public Library stands). Carnegie attended the official opening — the only time he attended the opening of any of the Ontario libraries he funded.

Fortunately, Carnegie didn't notice the building's one big faux pas. Instead of bearing the name Carnegie Library, the building had the title "Ottawa Public Library." To distract Carnegie's attention, a Union Jack Flag was placed in front of the title.

CROSSROADS

Daniel O'Connor, merchant, county treasurer and justice of the peace, was an early resident of Ottawa. O'Connor was an Irish Catholic who operated a store on Wellington Street in Upper Town —O'Connor Street in Ottawa is named after him. Sparks Street (named after Nicholas Sparks) and O'Connor Street intersect at right angles, in the form of a cross. This symbolizes the (hoped for) peace between Bytown's Orange and Green factions. O'Connor also holds one other

Did you know...

. . . that in 1950 John Hopps invented the first heart pacemaker in a National Research Council lab in Ottawa?

THEN AND NOW

important distinction. He and his wife Margaret were the parents of a daughter, Mary, the first white child born (1827) in the town.

HOCKEY TOWN

Although the current incarnation of the NHL's Ottawa Senators began in 1992, Ottawa's hockey history goes back to 1891. Between 1891 and 1902, teams sponsored by local businesses began playing throughout the city. Prominent early teams included the Rideau Rebels, the Ottawa Electrics, Enright's Boarders, the Bronsons, the Ottawa University team, and, most famously, the Ottawa City Hockey Club (later known as the "Silver Seven" and then the Senators).

Ottawa would bring home its first Stanley Cup in 1903. The team's rise that year coincided with the arrival of a rookie named Frank McGee. Although McGee would only play four seasons before retiring at age 24, in that short time he became hockey's first superstar, leading the team to four straight Stanley Cup championships.

In 1917, the Ottawa Senators became (along with the Montreal Canadiens, Montreal Wanderers and Toronto Arenas) charter members of the newly formed National Hockey League. During the NHL's first decade, they would finish first seven times and win four Stanley Cups on their way to becoming the league's first dynasty.

The Senators' stint in Ottawa ended in 1934 when the Senators moved to St. Louis, before completely folding the following year. No team would come close to matching the Senators' success until the Maple Leafs won five Stanley Cups in the 1940s.

Since their return to the NHL in 1992, the Senators have not yet won the Stanley Cup. They qualified for the playoffs in the 2014-15 season, but lost to the Montreal Canadians in the first round of playoffs.

Did you know...

. . . that James Naismith, the inventor of basketball, was an Ottawa Valley boy from nearby Almonte, Ontario?

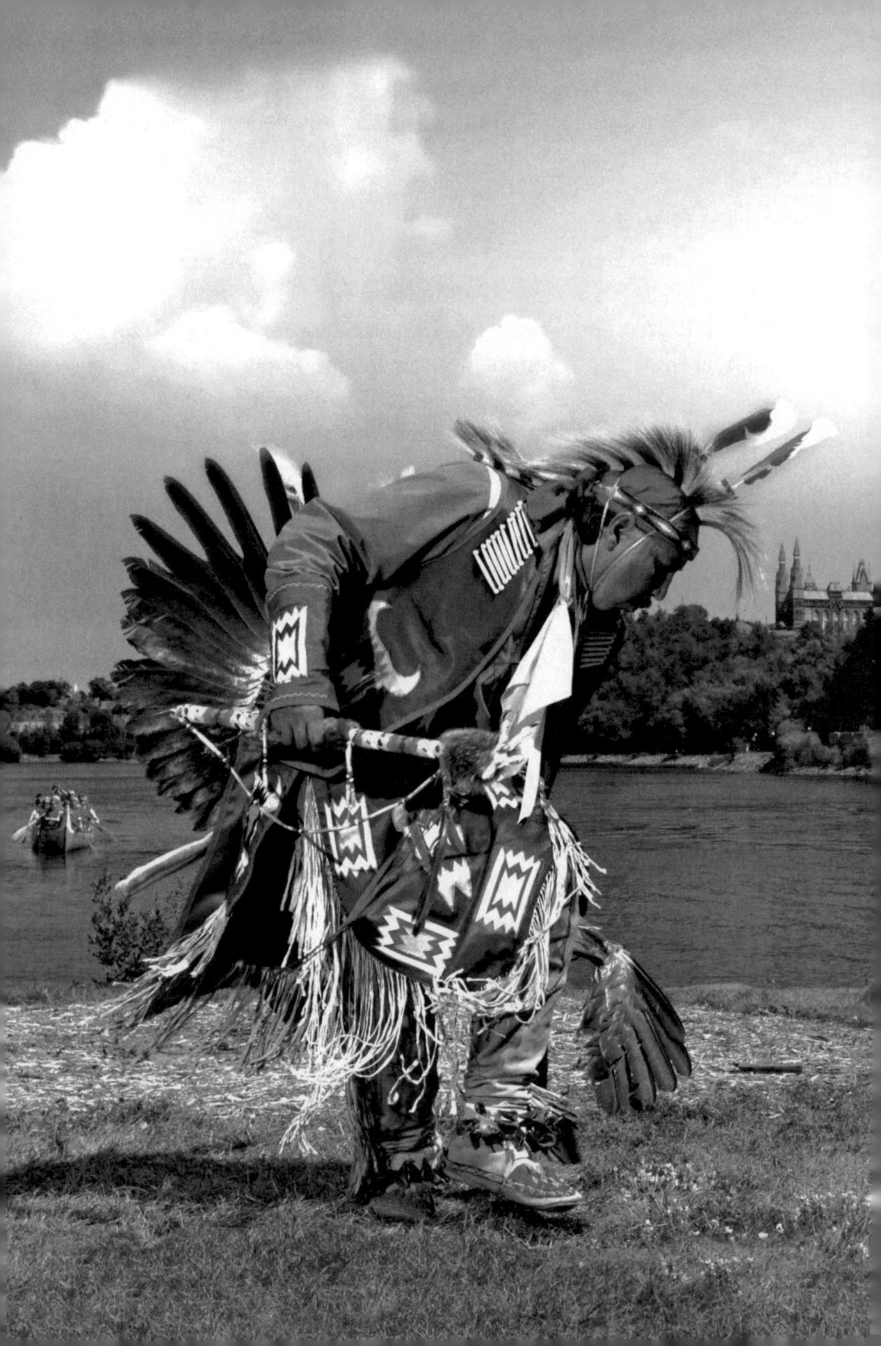

FIRST PEOPLE

The First People

Algonquin oral history indicates the Algonquin migrated to the Ottawa River Valley from the Atlantic coast. Archaeological evidence shows that Aboriginal people were in the area at least 8,000 years before the Europeans reached Canada's shores.

The Algonquin were once the largest and most widespread of Aboriginal groups. The most powerful of the Algonquin were the Kichesipirini, or "people of the great river," who were stationed at Alumette Island. When the Europeans arrived their position at the mouth of the Ottawa River enabled them to assert a level of control over the fur trade.

In 1570, the Algonquin were embroiled in a bitter war against the Iroquois. It was a war that continued well after the first recorded meeting between the Kichesipirini and Samuel de Champlain at Tadoussac in 1603. Because of their control over the fur trade, Champlain sided with the Algonquin, supplying them with French weaponry that proved instrumental in winning a 1609 battle with the Iroquois.

When the Algonquin and their Montagnais allies were faced with a serious attack by the Huron some twenty years later, this time the French were not around to help them. (The French were now dealing with Britain in a battle for a continent.) As a further threat to the

Algonquin monopoly over the fur trade, Dutch settlers were now providing the Mohawk with firearms.

The pressure from their rivals greatly weakened the once powerful band and they were eventually pushed out of the lower Ottawa River and into French areas such as Montreal and Trois-Rivieres. By the late 1660s, when the French signed a peace treaty with the Iroquois that provided for protection for their allies, war and disease had left only an estimated 2,000 (Christian) Algonquin to return to the northern Ottawa Valley.

POPULATION

Almost 250,000 Aboriginal people live in Ontario with more than 40,000 living in the Ottawa-Gatineau metropolitan area. This is a sweeping increase from 1981, when less than 4,000 Aboriginal people called the city of Ottawa home.

Of this population, the majority identify as a North American Indian, less than 8,000 as Métis and a handful are Inuit. Barely a third of those who identify as Aboriginal people have registered Indian status but this is not unique to Ottawa. Nationwide, less than half of the country's Aboriginal population are registered Indians.

Source: Statistics Canada.

ABORIGINAL POPULATION BREAKDOWN

Age	Population	% of Aboriginal Population	% Total City Population
0-14	4,160	20.2	.37
15-24	3,605	17.5	.32
25-54	10,180	49.4	.90
55-64	1,655	8.0	.15
65+	995	4.8	.09

MEDIAN AGE OF OTTAWA'S ABORIGINALS

- Male: 34.1
- Female: 34.2

CHIEF TESSOUAT:
THE ONE-EYED RULER

Being blind in one eye did nothing to slow Chief Tessouat from making his mark on history. The leader of the powerful Kitchesipirini nation on Alumette Island, near present-day Pembroke, Tessouat met Samuel de Champlain at Tadoussac in 1603 – the first recorded contact between Europeans and the Algonquin. Tessouat's party and their allies were celebrating their recent victory over the Iroquois, with whom they were embroiled in a long-standing war.

An ambitious and strong-willed man, Tessouat's tribe had exerted a great deal of power over the Ottawa River due to their strategic position at the mouth of the river. He imposed tolls on other groups that passed through to trade at Montreal and was even successful in preventing the French from exploring further upriver in 1613.

Champlain sent a young man named Nicholas de Vignau to live at Alumette with Tessouat's band during the winter of 1611-12 to learn the language and customs of the Algonquin. When he reported back to Champlain, he told him that he had traveled with the Algonquin to a "northern sea" (Hudson Bay). Not wanting to provide the English with an easier passage to the colony, Champlain wanted to claim the waters for France.

Champlain journeyed to Alumette in 1613 and asked Tessouat for guides through enemy Nipissing territory to this sea, but Tessouat told him that Vignau was lying about having left the camp during his stay and that no such body of water existed. Though Vignau took back his story, it may have been due to intimidation as opposed to it truly being a lie.

Tessouat also controlled his tribe's position as fur trade middlemen by spreading rumours in Huron country about Champlain looking for revenge for the death of a fellow Frenchman.

Unfortunately, this ambition had its consequences. In 1636, Tessouat approached other bands looking for allies for an attack against the Iroquois who had just killed more than 20 of his tribe members. He was turned down because of the extortionist practices he used in the fur trade.

Tessouat died later that year and was succeeded by his son Paul who, strangely enough, shared his father's blindness in one eye.

WORKFORCE
The Aboriginal population in Ottawa-Gatineau has a 66 percent employment rate with the total average income clocking in at $35,508. The most commonly held occupations are in the areas of business, finance and administration.

Source: Statistics Canada.

LANGUAGE
Historically, the Aboriginal community in what is now the Ottawa area spoke various Algonquin dialects. Algonquin was the most widely spoken Aboriginal language group in North America, something the French recognized quickly when they arrived. They would often send someone from their group to live with the Algonquin to learn the language, which would prove invaluable in communicating with multiple Aboriginal groups.

While almost half of Ottawa's Aboriginal population can speak both official languages, only five percent have knowledge of an Aboriginal language. An even smaller percentage still speak their language at home.

- Percentage of Ottawa Aboriginal people whose first learned language was Aboriginal and who still understand this language: 5.4
- Percentage of Aboriginal population who speak Aboriginal languages at home: 3.9
- Percentage with knowledge of Aboriginal languages: 6.1

SPEAKING THE LANGUAGE:
Hello – Kwey kwey
Man – Ininì
Woman – Ikwe
Great River – Kichi Sibi
Human being – Anishinabe
How are you? – Ki mino kidjebawak
Good morning – Mino kidjebawak

FIRST PEOPLE

Be good – Mino ya win
What's happening? – Anez duz
What are you doing later? – Andi e ijitaian nanage
Who are you? – Awenen dash kin
Wake up – Wanishkan
Dog – Animosh
Birds – Pinisheezh
Deer – Wawashkeshi
Beaver – Amik
Sun – Kìzis
Moon – Tibik-kìzis
Water – Nibì
Eat – Mìdjin
See – Wàbi
Hear – Nòndam
Sing – Nigamo

Source: Native American Language Net; Eagle Village First Nation.

CREATION MYTH: SIBLING RIVALRY

According to Algonquin beliefs, Mother Earth had two sons named Glooskap and Malsum. When their mother died, Glooskap, who was good and creative, created plants, animals and people from his mother's body.

Meanwhile, the evil and destructive Malsum made poisonous plants and snakes. Malsum soon tired of his brother's goodness and plotted to kill him. Malsum bragged to Glooskap about his own invincibility — even though he could be killed by a fern root — and nagged him to reveal where his vulnerability lay.

Since Glooskap was unable to lie, he revealed that only the feather of an owl could kill him. Malsum then made a dart with an owl's feather and killed his brother. Since the power of good was so strong, however, Glooskap was resurrected and he realized that he needed to get rid of his brother for the survival of the creatures he created.

One day Glooskap lured his brother to a stream by saying a

Take 5: CHIEF KIRBY WHITEDUCK'S TOP FIVE HISTORICAL CLAIMS TO ALGONQUIN TERRITORY

Kirby Whiteduck is currently a two-term Chief of the Algonquins of Pikwakanagan First Nation. He has earned his Honours Bachelor of Arts (Social Anthropology) from York University and is the author of the book *Algonquin Traditional Culture*. The Pikwakanagan Indian Reserve at Golden Lake is 90 miles west of Ottawa in the heart of Algonquin territory.

1. In July of 1833, the Algonquin Grand Chief Pierre Louis Constant Pynency, along with 15 other Algonquin Chiefs petition Lord Aylmer, the Governor of Lower Canada for land: "Read the history of the last war. Who went first to the (American) border and faced the enemy? It was us the Algonquin and Nipissings who defended this land that we are asking you for today. . . Other nations have done practically nothing, some were traitors to our father and they have been generously rewarded with lands. But for us what have you done? Promises only. Perhaps, my father, some evil birds have advised you to do otherwise, have told you to grant nothing to the Algonquins and Nipissings. . . grant them what they ask, land along Ottawa or on the rivers that flow into it, that this land may belong to us, that we may be free there, to hunt and fish there without anyone preventing us from doing so."

2. In July of 1838 the Grand Chief Jean Baptist Keijico- Manitou along with 16 other Algonquin and Nipissing Chiefs and War Chiefs state in a petition to the Colonial Government;
"Tell our father who we are. Tell him his children, the Nipissings and Algonquins, have always been loyal subjects, that his predecessors our Fathers, always found us ready to follow their commands. We have spilled our blood for our King and our country. And we are prepared to do so again, at any time. . ."

3. In a Council proceeding in September of 1841 between the Principal Chiefs of the Algonquins and Nipissings and representatives of the governments' Indian Department the Grand Council Chief Francois Kaondinoketch states to the Indian Department representatives that;"During the last two wars with the United States, our

FIRST PEOPLE

ancestors as well as ourselves, were called upon by our Fathers, the then Governors and told that we had lands to defend, as well as our White Brethren. We obeyed. We knew it was our duty to defend our hunting grounds. We gave the War Whoop. We fought and bled, in defending the rights of our great Father the Governor-General, that we are ready to do so again whenever called upon."

4. In a 1847 petition to the Right Honourable James Bruce, the Governor General of British North America, the Algonquin and Nipissing state; "At the beginning of the revolutionary war with the Big Knives (Americans) our Great Father the King required the assistance of his Red Children the Algonquins and Nipissings. Our ancestors were told by his representative that we were called upon as allies of our Great Father to encounter the enemy that we had the Honor to defend our lands and families, and must act in concert with our white brethren. We were no sooner summoned then the war whoop reiterated in our camp. We remembered what our Great Father the King had done for us and our ancestors. We fought and bled for our Father and Country, we did the same in the last war with the Big Knives, and in a similar case we are ready to do it again."

5. In March of 1983, well over a century later, the Algonquins of Pikwakanagan led by Chief Cliff Meness still recall the continued fidelity and commitment to the Crown and still ask for justice and recognition of ownership of land and resources in Algonquin unsurrendered traditional territory. Chief Meness along with over 100 other Pikwakanagan members state; "That in performance of our Treaty obligations to the Crown we have taken up arms in every war in which our services have been requested. Our warriors have served with distinction in the War of the American Revolution, the War of 1812, and most recently the two World Wars. In the First World War every man of Golden Lake volunteered and served in the army. None of these wars were our own. We shed our blood only to keep our promises to the Crown."

flowering reed could also kill him. Once there, he uprooted a fern and threw it at Malsum, killing him. Malsum's spirit was banished underground where it became a wolf-spirit that occasionally torments humans and animals at night.

LIFESTYLE

The Algonquin were semi-nomadic people. For the greater part of the year, they lived in family groups consisting of the grandparents, mother, father, children and adopted children. They had a regular cycle of travel that took them to a large river or lake in the summer where they would meet up with other families.

During this social community time, marriages were arranged and the tribes were often visited by European traders and missionaries. Due to their traveling, their material possessions were limited to what they could carry with them in a canoe or toboggan, including hunting materials and clothing.

The Algonquin were excellent hunters and trappers. They relied mainly on fish and game such as moose, black bear and beaver for food. The animals also supplied them with clothing, raw materials for tools and later furs as a means of obtaining European goods.

WHAT'S IN A NAME?

The Algonquin name comes from a Malecite word, meaning "our relatives." Due to their position on the highly commercial Ottawa River, the Algonquin were often referred to as "adawe" or traders.

FIRST PEOPLE

They Said It

> "*He replied that he had promised something impossible for him, since he had never seen the sea, and that the desire of making the journey had led him to say what he did, also that he did not suppose I would undertake it. . .*"
> – Samuel de Champlain, recounting Nicholas Vignau's reason for lying about traveling to see Hudson Bay with the Algonquin.

OTTAWA RIVER

The Ottawa River was the most direct trading route between the St. Lawrence River and groups who lived further inland. Called the Kichi sibi, or the Great River, by the Algonquin, the waterway became the main route in the development of the fur trade.

There are a couple of different theories as to how the river received its present name. Some say it was named after the Algonquin. Others attribute the name to the Odawa, an Aboriginal group who lived by Lake Huron, but were such frequent trade visitors that they became synonymous with the Algonquin and the river.

STAKING THEIR CLAIM

Since 1983, status and non-status Algonquin have been embroiled in negotiations over their rights to land. Unlike large parts of Canada, the land on which Ottawa was built was not allotted through a treaty with the first inhabitants.

Algonquin therefore say they still have Aboriginal rights and ownership of the land and its natural resources. The claim, which covers 36,000 square km, is the one of the most extensive in Ontario.

Take 5 — FIVE GOVERNMENT OBJECTIVES IN THE ALGONQUIN LAND CLAIM NEGOTIATIONS

1. To avoid creating injustices for anyone in the settlement of the claim.
2. To protect the rights of private landowners, including their access to and use of their land.
3. To establish certainty and finality with respect to title, rights and interests in the land and natural resources with the intention of promoting stability within the area and increasing investor confidence.
4. To identify and protect Algonquin rights.
5. To enhance the economic opportunities of the Algonquin with the intention of also benefiting and promoting general economic and commercial opportunities in the area.

Source: Ontario Secretariat for Aboriginal Affairs.

ON RESERVE

Today, there are 10 groups of status Algonquin in Canada, only one of which lives in Ontario. The rest are in Quebec. The Algonquins of Pikwàkanagàn live on Golden Lake reserve, about an hour and a half west of Ottawa. Pikwàkanagàn means "beautiful hilly country covered in evergreens."

The reserve was formed on 1,561 acres in 1873 following an appeal to the Governor General from five families for 200 acres each. As of May 2007, Pikwàkanagàn has a population of 414 living on the reserve and a total registered community of 1,948.

Sources: Algonquins of Pikwakanagan; Indian and Northern Affairs Canada.

SPIRITUALITY

The Algonquin belief system is centred around a Creator with whom they are encouraged to create their own unique relationship. They believe that everything is connected and so they take only what they need from the land.

FIRST PEOPLE

Take 5 FIVE ABORIGINAL HEADQUARTERS IN OTTAWA

1. **Assembly of First Nations** A national organization that represents all First Nations citizens.
2. **Métis National Council** A group that represents the Métis at a national level.
3. **Congress of Aboriginal Peoples** Represents interests of off-reserve Aboriginal people.
4. **Native Women's Association of Canada** A group that works to improve the social, economic and political well-being of Aboriginal women.
5. **Inuit Tapiriit Kanatami** A national organization representing Canada's Inuit population.

SMUDGING CEREMONY

The smudging ceremony is a cleansing ritual used before Algonquin spiritual gatherings to help participants get into the necessary calmness.

To begin, a ball of dried plants held in a shell or bowl is lit with a fire and left to smolder. The smoke this produces is pushed forward with the feather of an eagle and participants use the smoke to cleanse their hands as if washing them. Then, the smoke is pulled over one's heart, mouth, eyes, ears, lower back and feet.

The plants normally used for a smudging are chosen for their specific spiritual properties.

Tobacco is believed to open the door between our world and the spiritual one. Sage is supposed to reduce or eliminate negative energy. Cedar is for protection and grounding, while sweetgrass attracts positive energy.

ABORIGINAL PLACE NAMES
Kanata: Huron word meaning 'settlement' or 'village'
Manotick: Ojibwa word meaning 'island in the river'
Katimavik: Inuktitut word meaning 'meeting place'

Take 5 — FIVE PHILOSOPHIES
OF THE ANISHINABE WAY TO LIVE

1. Treat the Earth, and all that dwell upon it, with respect
2. Do what you know to be right
3. Dedicate a share of your efforts to the greater good
4. Take full responsibility for your actions
5. Remain close to the Great Spirit

Source: Algonquins of Pikwakanagan.

VICTORIA ISLAND

Located in the Ottawa River just west of Parliament Hill, Victoria Island has been important to the Algonquin people for centuries. Pre-contact, it was a permanent settlement used for trading with other First Nations people, and in the 17th century became a trading post. The island was also a spiritual site, used for gatherings and healing ceremonies.

Early settlers colonized the island to take advantage of the energy generated by the Chaudière Falls and the Aboriginal inhabitants were moved inland. The property was reclaimed in the 1960s by local Aboriginal groups and the land, which was essentially an industrial wasteland, was cleaned up and transformed into park land by the federal government.

The island is now home to Aboriginal Experience, a tourist attraction that boasts a mixture of tradition and contemporary Aboriginal culture. During the summer, visitors can tour a recreation of a traditional Aboriginal village, watch traditional dances and take part in a teepee retreat in the Gatineau hills or craft workshops. The site receives between 12,000 and 15,000 visitors every season.

Did you know...

. . . that the first female Algonquin chief in Canada, Anna Whiteduck, was elected in 1959 at the Pikwàkanagàn reserve?

FIRST PEOPLE

STEPPING INTO THE PAST:
THE CANADIAN MUSEUM OF CIVILIZATION

Located in Gatineau, just across the river from Parliament Hill, the Canadian Museum of Civilization showcases First Nations History and Culture.

The museum's First Peoples Hall is a must-see for those interested in getting up close with Canada's Aboriginal past. The permanent exhibit displays artifacts, documents and audiovisual presentations from Aboriginal groups across the country.

These include items such as original maps by Samuel de Champlain marking the location of the Algonquin in the Ottawa Valley and weapons used in the Algonquin's conflicts with the Iroquois. The museum's architecture, designed by noted Aboriginal architect Douglas J. Cardinal, is even modeled after Aboriginal beliefs. Built with the simple lines and forms that make up Aboriginal designs, the building was made to symbolize the relationship of humans to the land.

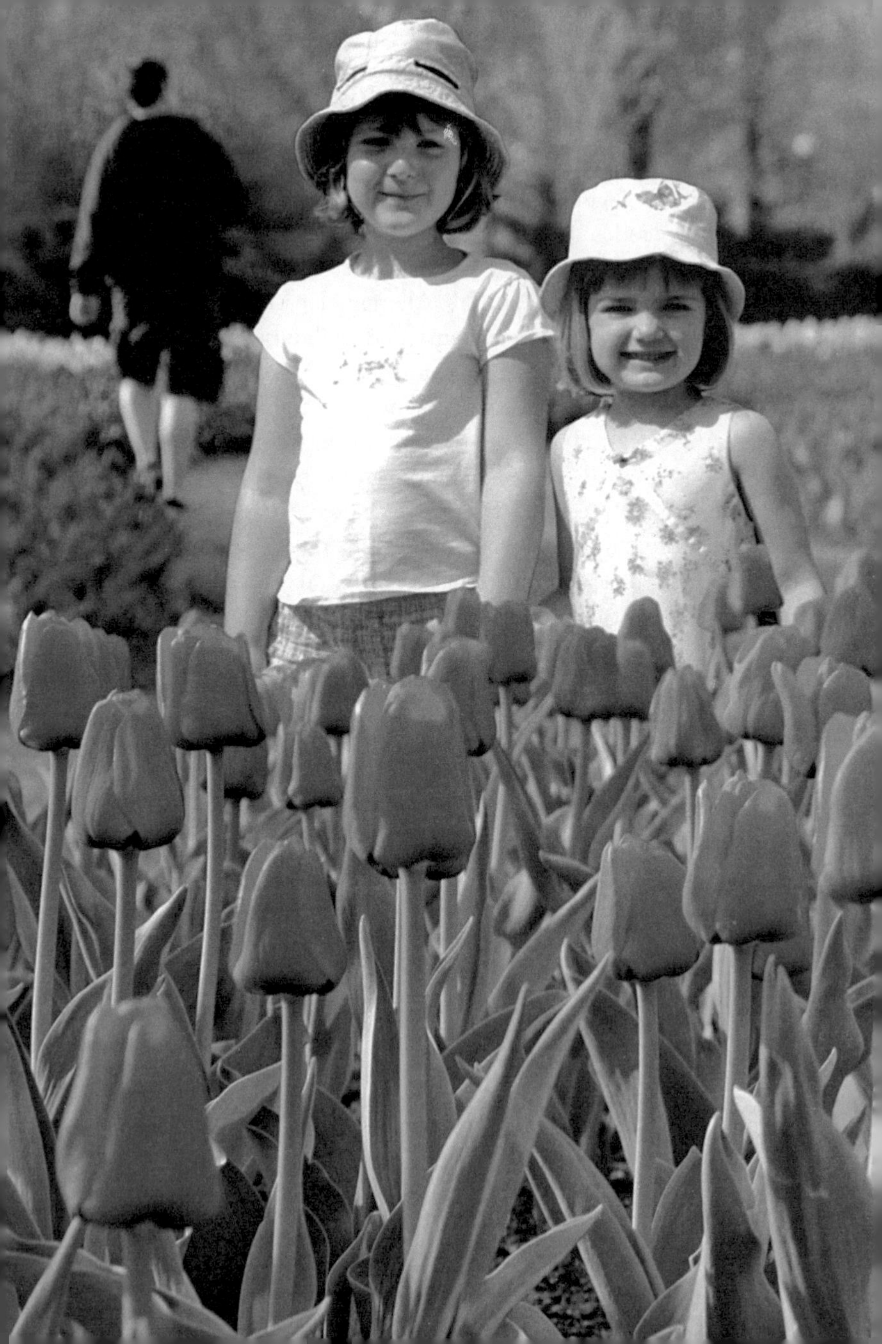

TAKE FIVE

Go Ahead, Take Five More

As you can probably tell, we are partial to things you can count on one hand. This chapter is more of that. It is designed to be fun, entertaining and insightful, not only in details about the city, but also about the person making the choices. It is a chapter that could have continued well beyond the bounds of this book. Ottawans, famous and not so famous, were literally bursting at the seams with opinions about their city.

BEN MULRONEY'S FIVE THINGS YOU DON'T KNOW ABOUT 24 SUSSEX DRIVE

Ben Mulroney, son of former Prime Minister Brian Mulroney, lived at 24 Sussex Drive from 1984 to 1993. He hosts the CTV program Canadian Idol and co-hosts CTV entertainment show eTalk.

1. My brother Mark and I lost a near-mint condition 1957 Mickey Mantle baseball card somewhere in the house. If you find it, I want it back.

2. Margaret Trudeau named the sitting room on the second floor "the Freedom Room." As far as I know, the name is still being used today.

3. There's a secret safe on the first floor, behind a painting. In eight years, I never saw it opened. I don't think anyone actually knows the combination.

4. The walls, floors and ceilings are very, very thin. If you are asleep on the second floor, you will hear everything on the third floor.

5. I went back to 24 in 2006 for the first time in years, and the combination lock that leads to the pool had not been changed.

FIVE BEST HOCKEY PLAYERS BRIAN KILREA'S EVER COACHED:

Brian Kilrea is an Ottawa legend. Part of a family with deep roots in NHL and Ottawa hockey, "Killer" has coached the OHL's Ottawa 67s for a remarkable 31 years. He is the first OHL coach to win 1,000 games and to coach 2,000 games. Ottawans love "Killer" because he's not only produced consistently successful teams (the 67s have missed the playoffs only once during his tenure), but he has, with the exception of a 2 year stint as Assistant Coach with the New York Islanders, spurned numerous NHL offers to remain in his hometown.

1. **Bobby Smith**
2. **Doug Wilson**
3. **Tim Higgins**
4. **Andrew Cassels**
5. **Jim Fox**

TAKE FIVE

BRIAN KILREA'S FIVE BEST NHL PLAYERS FROM OTTAWA
1. **Denis Potvin**
2. **Bobby Smith**
3. **Doug Wilson**
4. **Larry Robinson**
5. **Steve Yzerman**

MICHAEL HAYNES' FIVE FAVOURITE HIKING TRAILS BY SEASON

Michael Haynes moved to Ottawa in 2003 and immediately began hiking the many trails of the region. He also began profiling regional outdoor activities on CBC Radio. He has published numerous hiking guides for Atlantic Canada, and his *Hiking Trails of Ottawa* will be released in spring 2008.

1. **Spring:** Parc national de Plaisance, located about 70 km east of Ottawa on the Ottawa River, is the perfect spot to enjoy the riot of spring flowers and returning birds. The park's 14 km of trails provide excellent viewing of the more than 100,000 Canada Geese that migrate through its bays and marshes from late April to mid May. Plus, you can take a ferry ride between the two halves of the park. How special is that?

2. **Summer:** Ordinarily, when temperatures are sweltering, hiking is not uppermost in many people's minds. The Ottawa River Pathway, which extends from Orléans to Rockcliffe Park, offers the opportunity to find relief next to the river's moderating influence. And, if the breezes aren't refreshing enough, you can always find safe places to jump into the river.

3. **Autumn:** When the hardwoods of Gatineau Park change their green summer uniform for the more colourful hues of autumn, tens of thousands flock to the crest of the Eardley Escarpment for the view. The 2.5 km-long trail on King Mountain is the most popular hike. The mountain stands slightly higher than surrounding hills, and has ten viewing sites. Hint: be there shortly after dawn and you may have the hill to yourself.

4. **Winter:** If you enjoy a challenging snowshoe with the reward of superb views, then there is no better trail available than the Wolf Trail in Gatineau Park. Rugged, hilly, and, at 8.5 km, fairly long, this trail begins and ends on the shores of Meech Lake. In between you climb to the top of the escarpment overlooking the Ottawa River Valley. Magnificent, even at -30°C.

5. **Year-Round:** The Slide Lake Loop in Frontenac Provincial Park near Kingston is a gem that is worth the trip. At 21 km, it is a little long for most to complete in one day, but there are numerous campsites. For a 3 km walk, try the Doe Lake Loop. The park is an exceptional wilderness preserve that I enjoy more with each visit.

ART MONTAGUE'S FIVE BEST KEPT OTTAWA SECRETS

A self-confessed political junkie, Art Montague was deeply involved in west end Ottawa community development. At the turn of the millennium he made a decision to take up his pen and resume writing as a full-time career. Four books and literally hundreds of articles later, he hasn't had time to look back. Every political city has its secrets, says Montague, and not all of them are political. That, he says, is a good thing.

TAKE FIVE

1. The best Chinese restaurant in Ottawa isn't in the Somerset Street Asian district. Inscrutable Chinese gourmands most often gather at the **Won Ton House** on Wellington Street in Westboro.

2. Take a doggie bag if you go to eat at **Monkey Joe's** on Carling Avenue. Here plates are usually platters heaped higher than a trencherman's groaning board, and not a morsel should be wasted. Lots of stuff, good stuff, fill up, burp and ask to take the rest home with you. Friendly staff will oblige with a smile.

3. Stomach full, a stroll may be in order. Over in Gatineau, tucked on the Ottawa River near the Museum of Civilization is **Brebeuf Park**. This patch of wilderness is a waterfowl watcher's Eden, plus it provides the best view of Chaudiere Falls available either side of the Ottawa River.

4. Who would have thought the **National Library of Canada** is not only the best library in the country, its staff will work hard to find just about anything Canadian that's in hard copy? The big secret is the library's photo collection, probably started about the same time the camera was invented. Incidentally, most of the government ministries have their own libraries, which the general public is welcome to browse—not in the stacks, but on computer for call-up of individual items.

5. "If I tell you, I'll have to kill you." This secret cannot be revealed: Everyone thinks Ottawa's **Elvis Sighting Society** holds its meetings at Moe Atallah's Newport Restaurant or maybe behind the restaurant in Elvis Lives Lane. However, these are dedicated serious-minded people, pillars of Ottawa society, though some are media people. More likely they meet someplace where they can actually sight Elvis. Seems reasonable, but they're not saying. Ask a member of the Society and all you'll get for a response is an Elvis patented gyration and an "Uh, Huh!"

BARB FRADKIN'S FIVE MURDER SCENARIOS IN THE NATION'S CAPITAL

Nationally acclaimed mystery writer Barbara Fradkin not only makes her home in Ottawa, she also sets her dark tales of murder here. In 2005 and again in 2007, her novels won the Crime Writers of Canada Arthur Ellis Award for Best Novel. She has also been a three-time nominee for the Arthur Ellis Best Short Story Award. By 2014, there were ten novels in the Inspector Green series. "None so Blind" was published in 2014. "Fire in the Stars" is her most recent novel and was published in 2016.

1. **Crossing the dance floor.** Deserting the ranks to join the other team is a hanging offence, particularly if the home team is down a few men. There will always be plenty of loyal team players eager to bump the defector off, primarily because they see their own chances for stardom go up in smoke.

2. **Playing with whistles.** The mere act of brandishing a whistle is enough to put a price on the holder's head. Public disgrace looms, careers hover on the brink, and prison beckons — powerful motives indeed for silencing the blower before he can raise that whistle to his lips.

3. **Playing with imaginary friends.** This was a favourite game of corporate and political pals in recent years, until the aforementioned whistle blowers spoiled the game. Huge sums of money change hands, often in envelopes under the table, for imaginary services rendered, through contracts written in invisible ink, by people no one can remember.

4. **Forgetting official p's and q's.** Language is serious business in Ottawa. There is always some zealot lurking in the shadows, eager to count the number of French and English words in a politician's speech, or to quibble with the translation of Page 265 of the Saskatoon Workplace Green Algae Reduction Plan. Suspects can come from both extremes of the language divide and need no motive beyond the thrill of stirring each other up.

TAKE FIVE

5. **Designing a transit plan.** Lest visitors think the federal government is the only game in town, the municipal government has come up with a few of its own. One road to certain death is to submit a rapid transit proposal — any proposal — to city council.

TAKE 5: JACQUELIN HOLZMAN'S FIVE IMPORTANT DECISIONS THAT SHAPED OTTAWA

Jacquelin Holzman was the 55th Mayor of Ottawa (1991 – 1997) and is the co-author with Rosalind Tosh of *Ottawa: Then & Now*

1. In 1800, Philemon Wright walked up to Ottawa from Woburn, Massachusetts, the first of the immigrants who came to Ottawa. He started the lumber industry.

2. In 1820, the decision was made to build a canal from Kingston to Ottawa, running from Dow's Lake along what is now Preston Street to the Ottawa River. John LeBreton, who for 499 sterling had bought land over which this would run, offered it to the Earl of Dalhousie for six times that—our first land speculation. The Earl decided not to pay such an outrageous amount, and bought land at Entrance Bay instead. This decision moved the heart of Ottawa from where it might have been, well west of where the Parliament Buildings now stand, to the east.

3. In 1826, Lt.-Col. John By arrived to build the canal. Instead of the straight, simple canal with two locks of the original plan, he was presented with a winding route through the city, which dropped 80 feet to the Ottawa River at Entrance Bay. Because of this, we now have not only the Italian neighbourhood along Preston Street where the canal would have run, but also a canal that threads through the city, with the benefits of boating in the summer and skating in the winter.

4. In 1857, Queen Victoria selected Ottawa to be the nation's capital. Ottawa was everyone's second choice. Built around the lumber industry, it was ugly, rough and male-dominated. We went from white pine to bureaucracy and red tape.

5. The fifth decision was that taken by the immigrants who have come to Ottawa in Philemon Wright's footsteps. They are the ones who have built Ottawa and Canada.

RHYS PHILLIPS' TOP FIVE LANDMARK BUILDINGS

Rhys Phillips, an Ottawa architecture critic and Honorary Fellow of the Royal Architectural Institute of Canada, is the author of *National Capital Modern – Five Landmark Buildings*.

1. **Old CBC Headquarters**, now the Edward Drake Building, 1500 Riverside Drive (1964 CBC Design Department). If the so-called International Style was frequently elegant but bland, the CBC's own resident architect, D.G. McKinstry, embraced the former but eschewed the latter. Richly coloured Kingston limestone walls terminate the three parabolic curves of the Y-shaped building's glass and granite elevations, while a delicate flared roof and floating portico arch at the main entrance are anything but bland.

2. **Bank of Canada Building** (1979, Arthur Erickson Architect). In 1938, Canada ensconced its central bank in what seemed like an impenetrable strongbox of a building designed by architect S.G. Davenport. Four decades later, Canada's most famous modernist, Arthur Erickson, embraced this austere stone block with transparent glass arms detailed in finely crafted, pre-aged copper mullions.

TAKE FIVE

3. **Museum of Civilization** (1989, Douglas Cardinal Architect). More than a landmark, this iconic building can be read as either an organic yet manufactured piece of landscape, or as a mythic First Nations' creature of creation. Not incidentally, it superbly frames as its first exhibit the incomparable Library of Parliament across the Ottawa River.

4. **National Archives** (1997, IKOY Architects). This impressive "jewel box" is located on the Quebec side of the Ottawa river in Gatineau. It is a resolutely modernist interpretation of an ancient Doric temple and employs a remarkable skin of transparent glass stretched across towering but wonderfully detailed steel columns to shield a massive concrete mountain vault containing the nation's preserved memories.

5. **School of Information Technology and Engineering** (2002, IKOY Architects), located on the University of Ottawa campus. This second excellent and "green" building by IKOY's Ron Keenberg acts as a powerful high-tech gatepost to the National Capital. An abundant use of transparent glass, a robust layering of solid planes, and a composition of diverse forms ensures it is a landmark to rival those of the nearby Parliamentary precinct.